Makerspaces

PRACTICAL GUIDES FOR LIBRARIANS

About the Series

This innovative series written and edited for librarians by librarians provides authoritative, practical information and guidance on a wide spectrum of library processes and operations.

Books in the series are focused, describing practical and innovative solutions to a problem facing today's librarian and delivering step-by-step guidance for planning, creating, implementing, managing, and evaluating a wide range of services and programs.

The books are aimed at beginning and intermediate librarians needing basic instruction/guidance in a specific subject and at experienced librarians who need to gain knowledge in a new area or guidance in implementing a new program/service.

About the Series Editor

The **Practical Guides for Librarians** series was conceived by and is edited by M. Sandra Wood, MLS, MBA, AHIP, FMLA, Librarian Emerita, Penn State University Libraries.

M. Sandra Wood was a librarian at the George T. Harrell Library, the Milton S. Hershey Medical Center, College of Medicine, Pennsylvania State University, Hershey, Pennsylvania, for over thirty-five years, specializing in reference, educational, and database services. Ms. Wood worked for several years as a development editor for Neal-Schuman Publishers.

Ms. Wood received an MLS from Indiana University and an MBA from the University of Maryland. She is a fellow of the Medical Library Association and served as a member of MLA's board of directors from 1991 to 1995. Ms. Wood is founding and current editor of *Medical Reference Services Quarterly*, now in its thirty-fifth volume. She also was founding editor of the *Journal of Consumer Health on the Internet* and the *Journal of Electronic Resources in Medical Libraries* and served as editor/coeditor of both journals through 2011.

Titles in the Series

1. *How to Teach: A Practical Guide for Librarians* by Beverley E. Crane

2. *Implementing an Inclusive Staffing Model for Today's Reference Services* by Julia K. Nims, Paula Storm, and Robert Stevens

3. *Managing Digital Audiovisual Resources: A Practical Guide for Librarians* by Matthew C. Mariner

Makerspaces

A Practical Guide for Librarians

John J. Burke
Revised by Ellyssa Kroski

SECOND EDITION

PRACTICAL GUIDES FOR LIBRARIANS, NO. 38

ROWMAN & LITTLEFIELD
Lanham • Boulder • New York • London

sPublished by Rowman & Littlefield
A wholly owned subsidiary of The Rowman & Littlefield Publishing Group, Inc.
4501 Forbes Boulevard, Suite 200, Lanham, Maryland 20706
www.rowman.com

Unit A, Whitacre Mews, 26-34 Stannary Street, London SE11 4AB

British Library Cataloguing in Publication Information Available

Library of Congress Cataloging-in-Publication Data Available

ISBN 978-1-5381-0818-5 (pbk. : alk. paper) | ISBN 978-1-5381-0819-2 (ebook)

∞™ The paper used in this publication meets the minimum requirements of American
National Standard for Information Sciences—Permanence of Paper for Printed Library
Materials, ANSI/NISO Z39.48-1992.

Printed in the United States of America

Contents

Figures and Tables

⊙ Figures

⊚ Tables

Makerspace Profiles

Makerspace at Town 'N Country Regional Public Library, Tampa-Hillsborough County Public Library System, Tampa, FL

Imaginarium, Mead Public Library, Sheboygan, WI

Maker Studio, Springdale Public Library, Springdale, AR

STEAM Central, Stephens Central Library, Tom Green County Library System, San Angelo, TX

LibLab: Makerspace and Technology Learning Center at South San Francisco Public Library, San Francisco, CA

Maker Lab, Chicago Public Library, Chicago, IL

⑥ Academic Library Makerspaces

The MILL, University of Idaho Library, Moscow, ID

Makerspace at Lawrence University Seeley G. Mudd Library, Appleton, WI

Library Maker Services at Penfield Library, State University of New York at Oswego, NY

Studio, UTC Library, University of Tennessee at Chattanooga, TN

Innovation Lab and Makerspace, Shapiro Library, Southern New Hampshire University, Manchester, NH

Innovation @ the Edge and Innovation Hub, University of Oklahoma, Norman, OK

DeLaMare Science and Engineering Library, University of Nevada, Reno, NV

ACU Maker Lab, Abilene Christian University Library, Abilene, TX

Preface

Welcome to *Makerspaces: A Practical Guide for Librarians*! When I was asked to revise this book for a second edition, I was thrilled. John Burke's volume has easily been one of my favorite go-to resources for learning about makerspaces in libraries, and I particularly loved the format, which combined anecdotal profiles of library makerspaces with concrete data from a survey of the field.

Makerspaces are a great passion of mine, and revising this volume gave me the opportunity to reach out to other librarians who are currently working in these creative spaces. Additionally, the survey that informs much of this book was an exciting undertaking to assume as it provides a wealth of information and insight into what other libraries are offering as far as tools, technology, and programming, as well as funding sources that they have found.

What's New

- Results of the 2017 Makerspaces in Libraries Survey, including an appendix with all of the results and tables as well as lists in each chapter
- Eighteen brand-new library makerspace profiles providing advice and inspiration for how to create your own library makerspace
- All-new tables and charts with survey results indicating trends and technologies in library makerspaces
- Over twenty new images and figures illustrating maker tools and trends as well as library makerspaces in action
- Updates and additions to tools, techniques, and essential advice, such as new lists of actual grant and funding sources for library makerspaces
- A brand-new comprehensive bibliography of sources for more information
- A helpful index to topics discussed throughout the book

What's in This Book

- Chapter 1, "The Library as a Creation and Collaboration Space," and chapter 2, "The Maker Movement and Building Up a Making Mind-Set," discuss the history of the maker movement as a whole as well as the connection between the mission of libraries and the concept of making.

- Chapter 3, "An Overview of Makerspace Implementations," details how to plan and implement a library makerspace.
- Chapter 4, "What Will Patrons Make in Your Makerspace?" explores the vast array of different maker tools and technologies that may be found in library makerspaces.
- Chapter 5, "Budgeting for a Makerspace," discusses how to develop budgets and find funding to support a library makerspace.
- Chapters 6 through 10 discuss specific maker tools, techniques, and technologies such as audio, image, and video creation; crafts and artistic pursuits; electronics, robotics, and programming; 3D printing and prototyping; and lesser-known making.
- Chapter 11, "Approaches for Developing a Makerspace That Enables Makers," makes recommendations for providing engaging programming and activities as well as for managing the space.
- Chapter 12, "Remaking the Library? Tracking the Present and Future of Making in Libraries," provides a slew of recommended resources for you to stay aware of current developments in the field as well as social channels to reach out to and learn from others.
- The appendix includes the results from the 2017 Makerspaces in Libraries Survey.
- The bibliography provides additional sources for you to consult to learn more about this intriguing topic.

Makerspaces are a growing service in libraries, and I hope you find this revised edition as helpful as I found Burke's original title to be. Please let me know if you have questions or comments by e-mailing me at ekroski@gmail.com.

Acknowledgments

I would like to heartily thank all of the librarians who took part in the survey that informs much of this book, as well as the many amazing librarians who generously donated their time to contribute a profile of their library makerspace.

Ellyssa Kroski

CHAPTER 1

The Library as a Creation and Collaboration Space

MAKERSPACES, FAB LABS, HACKERSPACES—these are all monikers for today's new hubs of community creation and learning. They are places to invent, tinker, build, and explore among like-minded individuals and fellow enthusiasts. They are as much about the tools and equipment found therein as they are about the spirit of creativity and pursuit of knowledge that encompasses them. They can exist as dedicated spaces, as mobile or pop-up locations, or simply as maker-oriented activities, since they are less dependent on the actual space than they are about the endeavors and knowledge-seeking journeys involved. They are social spaces where makers can learn from the experience and know-how of their peers, yet at the same time they are individually focused by the desired outcome and interest of each maker. Increasingly, libraries have begun to transform their mission and their physical spaces to incorporate these new creative enterprises, partnering with their communities in pursuit of the act of making.

Libraries serve a variety of purposes: maintainer of local information sources, community meeting space, study zone, and connector of people and information of all kinds.

Many of the library's core functions have centered on giving people access to materials that they could not find or afford on their own. As many books and other resources have become available in digital form, libraries have changed their spaces to accommodate uses beyond physical item storage: from collaborative study spaces to meeting areas to more space for computers. This trend of reshaping library spaces may have one more turn to take—one that tilts the work of libraries from information consumers and providers to information creators.

⊚ Definitions

Fab labs: spaces focused on prototyping physical products and designs using a combination of digital and physical tools

Hackerspaces: spaces initially focused on computer programmers and hackers as a place to share computers, socialize, and collaborate

Makerspaces: spaces used by people to share tools, knowledge, and ideas

Source: *Wikipedia,* s.v. "Fab Lab," June 7, 2017, https://en.wikipedia.org/wiki/Fab_lab; *Wikipedia,* s.v. "Hackerspace," June 7, 2017, https://en.wikipedia.org/wiki/Hackerspace.

What if a library had an area in it where patrons could make something? More than just a computer lab, where students write research papers and adults build résumés or where anyone can create a presentation with cloud-based software; instead, a space that is dedicated to both the tools for making and the discovery of talents for creativity and design, where people can make digital or physical items using tools and equipment that they do not own and where they can receive guidance on using them. This takes libraries on a path related to their traditional role of sharing expensive resources to increase knowledge, but this time toward releasing the potential of patrons to create. By providing the space and the means of making, libraries can spur learning, invention, creativity, and innovation.

Defining the Makerspace

Finding a definition for the concept of makerspaces is much akin to the blind men who attempted to identify an elephant. For them, the impression gained from feeling a part of the creature was taken to be indicative of its entirety. The man who touched the tail judged that the elephant was very much like a rope, while the man who encountered the trunk believed the elephant to be like a snake. Every man was correct in part but missed the larger picture and the larger truth, not to mention the size of the elephant.

So, too, can the makerspace be defined in ways that are driven by limited experience and that do not give the observer a full sense of what is possible. If a person imagines that makerspaces are all about 3D printers, then this is true in part. There are several makerspace applications for 3D printing: from prototyping models of products to re-creating historical artifacts to building replacement parts for a lawn mower out of plastic. If someone expects makerspaces to involve computer programming or robotics, then that view is also accurate to a degree. Programming and robotics work are happening in makerspaces for kids with LEGOs and for adults with a variety of devices. If an individual shares that makerspaces might have something to do with weaving or sculpture or welding, then those might also be valid conclusions. Unbelievable artwork and materials created by talented hands come from makerspaces that have potter's wheels, soldering, and looms. This train of *if*'s could continue ad nauseam, delineating all manner of technologies and creative arts. However, it is only fair to follow each *if* statement with a *but*: "but that is only one vision of what makerspaces can be."

This book delves into the evolving definition and potential of makerspaces at present and in the future. Upon completion, you will have an expanded and complete grasp of these entities. However, it is best to start with the basics and understand the nature of makerspaces at their most elemental before moving on to the larger picture. Cherie Bronkar said it well when she succinctly stated, "Makerspaces are, simply put, places where people gather to make things" (Bronkar, 2017: 3). Therefore, in order to make, a product must result from the work in the space.

⊚ Understanding the Development of Makerspaces

To understand how we got here, we must first take a look at how makerspaces came to be. The first thing that may come to mind is a laboratory, shop, or garage with an individual inventor or tinkerer, or perhaps a small team working and creating. This arrangement allows for easy access to tools and ideas with others. As well, the tools themselves provide the means for that inventor or group to bring an idea or discovery into being. We can picture the lone inventor coming out of nowhere with a product that fundamentally changes everything we know.

Getting those tools out into a common space where multiple inventors can come together and share their knowledge is an important breakthrough that makerspaces provide. The knowledge sharing becomes crucial and time-saving to those who hope to learn to make; yet, it also has a profound impact on those who know more but can still benefit from new perspectives and from the learning process that comes from teaching others.

This aspect owes its start to an earlier and continuing form of makerspace called the *hackerspace*. Hackerspaces are places that embrace a set of "hacker ethics," which include freedom, access, hands-on learning, and collaboration. They also support hacker activities that break down barriers and seek to repurpose objects and programs to do the unexpected (Clark, 2017: 287–288), all within a community and collaborative setting.

In addition to the community-sharing element of the makerspace, access to tools cannot be overstated. Individual inventors come from a range of economic classes, and they build their collections of machinery and tools to meet their own needs—from their own incomes. Gathering tools for common use or borrowing allows individuals to learn how to use them and make things with them without incurring excessive expenses along the way. Anyone might be able to compile a set of handy tools (e.g., hammers, screwdrivers, saws) over time at no more than a few tens of dollars per item. But purchasing a drill press, a laser cutter, or a 3D printer takes hundreds or thousands of dollars. Makerspaces allow for a big investment in equipment to be shared by many individuals, and those individuals have the freedom to experiment with equipment that they may or may

Figure 1.1. Noisebridge makerspace in San Francisco. *Image provided through a CC BY 2.0 License by Kyle Nishioka (madmarv00)*

not need until they find the right device to enable their making. You can see how the combination of tools might look in figure 1.1.

Describing Makerspaces

Now that we have established the two cornerstones of makerspaces—knowledge sharing and tool sharing—we can take a look at four other key characteristics of makerspaces, all of which are explored in the coming chapters.

Hands-On Learning and Exploration

Makerspaces may have classes to teach people how to use a particular tool or technology, but in general they are not home to a planned curriculum for learning. The goal of makerspaces is to provide the items and guidance needed to a maker so that one can explore and create at will. A maker starts with an idea, then follows through the process of creation oneself, with one's own hands.

Collaboration

Collaboration means working with others on projects. Perhaps you and others are working together on the same project or on separate projects but in the same place. It is drawn from the hackerspace model noted earlier. Working in a makerspace means working in an environment where you are not only formally taught by others but also inspired by their creations—and where you add your own inspiring reactions and comments to the loop of their creative processes.

> ### ◎ What Makerspaces Are Made Of
>
> Shared knowledge
>
> Shared tools
>
> Hands-on learning and exploration
>
> Coworking
>
> STEM education focus
>
> Maker culture—share your stuff!

STEM Education

STEM—science, technology, engineering, and mathematics—is an acronym used in schools and institutions of higher education to discuss the need for skills in the workforce that enable individuals to work with technologies and develop new ones. The United States, for instance, would like to enhance the STEM skills of its college graduates so that these individuals are more employable and can contribute to the country's future economic prosperity. Makerspaces have a focus on many of these same skills, and they can be a practical means of putting the theory of the classroom to work.

Maker Culture—Share Your Stuff!

The maker movement or maker culture (covered in detail in chapter 2) incorporates some of the shared knowledge–shared tool ethic discussed already. However, people who are engaged in making are also committed to sharing the designs that they used to create their products and projects. Having an open design culture means that Maker A can save time in her or his process by finding one or more models to guide the creation. She or he can also share ending project designs with Makers B and C and so on, thereby inspiring further making. The additive impacts of this openness are amazing, as we shall see.

◎ Making Products in Makerspaces

Makerspaces in libraries can be used to make all sorts of things. There is deeper coverage of this topic in the chapters ahead, but table 1.1 has a list of the most common tools or creation options available in library makerspaces, from an informal 2017 survey of 219 library makerspaces (see the appendix for details).

◎ Starting a Makerspace

A makerspace arises wherever making happens, which means that a flexible approach can be taken to budgeting for and developing one. A makerspace might be a large room filled with thousands of dollars' worth of 3D printers and digital fabrication machines along

Table 1.1. The Fifteen Most Common Technologies and Activities in Library Makerspaces (n = 219)

TECHNOLOGY/ACTIVITY	RESPONDENTS	
	%	N
Computer workstations	66.7	146
3D printing	65.8	144
Arts and crafts	64.8	142
Computer programming/software	48.4	106
3D modeling	46.6	102
Photo editing	45.2	99
Video editing	43.4	95
Tinkering	43.4	95
Arduino/Raspberry Pi	41.6	91
Robotics	36.5	80
Scanning photos to digital	33.8	74
Other (please specify)	33.3	73
Electronics	30.1	66
Fabric shop (sewing machines, leather sewing machines, CNC embroidery machines, etc.)	28.8	63
Vinyl cutting	25.6	56

with high-end computers, scanners, and other equipment. This setup might cost tens of thousands of dollars, not including the room in which, or the furniture upon which, the devices reside. A makerspace might also be a small collection of tools hung up on a wall in a meeting room or at one end of a library building, perhaps with a table dedicated for making activities. This option might cost a few hundred dollars to start, with raw materials added here and there over time.

Details on planning and budgeting are in chapter 5, but you must have four things to create a makerspace. First, your community has to have an interest in a makerspace: someone has to want to use it. Second, there has to be time available for someone in the library to heed the interest of the community and organize a response to it. Third, there has to be space available in the library to host maker activities, whether it is space shared with multiple activities or a dedicated room. Finally, there needs to be financial resources available—whether from grants, the library budget, or donations—to purchase equipment and supplies and to increase the available space, staff time, and interest (through marketing).

◎ Creating and Collaborating in Libraries

In today's changing world, libraries provide their patrons with a multitude of services, including a place to create and a place to talk. Yes, Ray Bradbury wrote *Fahrenheit 451* in the University of California, Los Angeles Library. We can point to countless examples of writers and scholars working on books and other publications at a table in a library. It is also true that much exchange of information comes through publications that often have some tie to the library; that is, authors do a lot of research in libraries, using library resources. Furthermore, books, DVDs, and other library items inspire a lot of people to study, create, invent, discover, and chronicle exciting things.

Makerspaces extend this capacity of sharing space and knowledge by increasing the types of work that can happen in a library. Now library patrons can see physical items appear from their labors rather than just words on a page. They can work with tools that take them from reading about robots to seeing them scoot across the floor. Patrons can hold the skull of a snake in their hands fresh from the 3D printer. They can also move from primarily consuming information in the library to making physical and virtual things there. A new world of creation awaits!

◎ Key Points

- Makerspaces are a combination of tools, an interested community of users, and a mind-set that provides for participants to teach one another and share their creations and ideas with the world.
- Makerspaces combine the characteristics of shared knowledge and tools with a focus on hands-on learning and exploration, a desire to cowork on projects alongside other makers, an attention to STEM education, and a dedication to the maker culture's ethos of sharing what is made with others.
- Makerspaces represent an intriguing opportunity for libraries to extend their mission of sharing resources with the widest audience possible to expand access and encourage learning.

◎ References

Bronkar, Cherie. 2017. "How to Start a Library Makerspace." In *The Makerspace Librarian's Sourcebook*, edited by Ellyssa Kroski, 3–28. Chicago: American Library Association, 2017.

Clark, Chad. 2017. "Library Hackerspace Programs." In *The Makerspace Librarian's Sourcebook*, edited by Ellyssa Kroski, 287–303. Chicago: American Library Association.

CHAPTER 2

The Maker Movement and Building Up a Making Mind-Set

MAKING IS NOT A NEW PHENOMENON; people have always made things. But the modern maker movement, fueled by recent technological advancements that have brought the tools of production within reach of consumers, is quite unique, as is the social aspect of the current movement, both online and within the spaces themselves. These advancements combined with the educational attributes of maker programming and activities have awakened a new and evolving maker culture that is best understood by reviewing the history of making.

⊚ Making as It Was

Making was never easy. Much time was spent coming up with an idea for a product, designing its form, imagining a method to create it, gathering materials and tools, and finally ending up with a finished product. The only way to make the process more efficient was to focus on a particular area of creation (e.g., blacksmithing, sewing, carpentry) and work at it over time to gain experience. This is not to say that all making in the past represented fine craftsmanship or was taken on only by specialists. Lots of needs were met over the centuries by people improvising solutions to situations to survive, whether in repairing structures, stitching fabric into clothing, or creating containers for food. Anyone could complete these same actions today with the same amount of skill and resources that their ancestors had, but imagine going the next step.

Producing something intricate, involved, and useful required great talent and the right tools. That talent could be gained only by a craftsperson working many years to learn the ins and outs of the trade. The tools could be hard to find. The slow pace of gaining skills made it difficult for innovative ideas to be brought to reality until the process could be learned. Practice and the right process led to the regular creation of items such as clocks, shoes, jewelry, and even foodstuffs such as grains. Once everything was in place, it could work well.

⊚ Making as It Has Been

However, making started to become easier in the late eighteenth century with the development of machinery that enabled greater volumes of products to be produced without the individual toil of multiple craftspeople. The factories that arose in the nineteenth century during the Industrial Revolution combined the activities of various crafts into a single location dedicated to turning raw materials into finished products. By using machinery and concentrating multiple talented individuals in one place, factories could more easily turn out large numbers of products and have a creative team fine-tune products and invent new ones. Eventually, trained operators could run machinery to churn out products of a quality and regularity that craftspeople of a century earlier could not have produced on their best day. The factory was typically owned by a small group of people who decided what would be produced and who employed dozens or hundreds of workers to make it happen.

This is effectively the world that we live in today. The products that society demands are designed, tested, focus-grouped, built, manufactured, and sold by a combination of businesses. Entry into this world of creators is relatively difficult without the capital to purchase or access equipment and machinery. For many individuals who have innovative or interesting ideas, the requirements for knowledge, tools, and the money to bring them all together are far too difficult.

⊚ Making as It Is Becoming

But what if something could be made without the maker knowing much about the process of creating that item? What if you could turn to groups of people, online and in person, who would share ideas and collaborate with you? What if an item could be produced without a factory full of expensive, specialized equipment? Or what if a product's design could be found online, modified, prototyped, and sent out for production or produced close at hand? Today, making and creating are no longer limited to the few individuals who can combine their desire to create with a team of designers and a factory full of tools. In fact, anyone can be a maker.

The Maker Movement

The surge of interest in creating physical items with digital tools and Internet-shared plans and techniques is known as the maker movement. The maker movement isn't an entirely new phenomenon as some aspects have their roots in the form of home hobbyists, arts and crafts groups, shop classes, practical education, and science fairs. Around 2005, when *Make:* magazine began publishing reports on different kinds of making and interesting projects to make, this activity was identified as an ongoing area of interest for a growing group of people. The publisher hosted the first Maker Faire in San Mateo, California, in 2006, which attracted over one hundred exhibitors. By the 2008 event, more than sixty-five thousand people attended the maker extravaganza (*Wikipedia*, 2017b). See figure 2.1 for a look inside Maker Faire. The movement was born, at least, as a collective concept.

One thing that has changed the process of making away from isolated, individual, small, or focused group efforts is the impact of collaboration among makers, often in a single space. It can be a group of people working on individual iterations of a similar type of project, or it can be individual artisans working with diverse media. The idea of co-working is one in which two or more individuals are working in the same physical space.

Figure 2.1. SparkFun Electronics at Denver Mini Maker Faire 2016. *Image provided through a CC BY 2.0 License by SparkFun Electronics, https://www.flickr.com/photos/sparkfun/27614201826/.*

They may be working on the same large project or on two or more different projects, but they can turn to one another for advice and suggestions. This mode of work is drawn from the example of hackerspaces mentioned in chapter 1, where programmers would gather in one space to share ideas and collaborate on projects. In the makerspace, there is enough space for work on design and physical creation using multiple types of media side by side. The paper artist and the metal sculptor can work alongside the programmer and the person crafting electronic devices.

The makerspace model was also heavily influenced by the creation of fab labs, led by Neil Gershenfeld of MIT's Center for Bits and Atoms. These labs, dedicated to the fabrication of items, consist of digital equipment for designing products and the digitally driven tools to create them (including laser cutters and computerized numerical control equipment). The concept caught on and has been replicated through the creation of hundreds of fab labs around the world, all of which operate with a common minimum equipment requirement and a shared mission. They were initially created for the rapid prototyping of products by local entrepreneurs, providing services not readily available in many parts of the world. They are also open to the general public and, while not centrally owned, must remain open to sharing ideas and activities with other fab labs.

Alongside and within the coworking and collaboration is a willingness to teach others. Makers who share space do not necessarily share an equivalence of talent. People come to the makerspace with a love for the creation of items and an acceptance of makers who may not know as much as they do. The environment is typically one of shared equipment and shared talents put to work on individual and shared creations. Perhaps it is better to frame this in terms of the people who come to the makerspace for the first time. What do they expect? They want to be inspired by the culture of making that pervades the space. They want to be able to use equipment or other tools that they cannot afford themselves. They want to learn new techniques from those in the makerspace so they can do what they love. They want to perhaps have their creations shaped by someone working in a completely different medium—perhaps a medium they might turn to themselves. This all requires a positive community environment.

Community is the defining element of the maker movement on both a local and international scale. Individuals must have a reason to cowork, something that motivates them to collaborate and share space. There is more coverage of ways to organize and select making oeuvres later in the book, but accept for now that makers are going to network only if they feel acceptance and a sense of peer bonding. This allows for the tremendous collaboration and training alluded to earlier.

⊚ Making and Learning

Making is not just a community event, though; it is also a chance for learning since a person can gain a strong educational impact from making. In the description of making, there is an allusion that connects the movement to education: that the community provides an instructional role for makers to learn from other makers. Makerspaces exist outside of classroom limitations, making these safe spaces that encourage learners to fail in their pursuit to explore ideas at their own pace while learning from their peers. "In an ideal educational makerspace, the line between 'student' and 'teacher' starts to blur through collaboration and mutual participation in projects. As learners encounter obstacles and challenges, their peers and collaborators can offer solutions, ideas, and advice—

effectively taking on the teaching role—in a fluid, constantly shifting process" (Costello, Powers, and Haugh, 2017: 36).

Participatory Culture

The first educational application of making relates to the concept of participatory culture. Participatory culture became quite pronounced with the advent of Web 2.0, during which time individuals traded in their passive roles as consumers of information for more active ones and became producers or contributors of information and content (*Wikipedia*, 2017d). For instance, we can see this idea in practice with YouTube. People watch commercially produced music videos, instructional videos, and episodes of television dramas, but they can also create their own videos and upload them. The same experience applies to a variety of Internet sites and mobile device apps in the creation and sharing of images, text, and videos online by the many as they also experience the more polished creations of the few. This idea of being a participant and creator has extended to areas beyond media. If applied to a wider view of the ways that human beings consume products, a similar move to self-creation or self-fabrication can be seen in the maker movement.

Learning is more than a by-product of self-fabrication. By putting the means of forming and shaping items into the hands of students, teachers allow for independent progress on building tasks. The benefits of spontaneous collaboration on projects can further put students in the role of teacher, giving them opportunities to examine and explain their practices. All of this imparts more understanding to students. At the very least, the freedom to participate in creation (whether digital or physical) puts tools in the hands of learners, which they can utilize beyond their immediate tasks.

Constructionism and Experiential Learning

The second application of making to education comes from the theory of constructionism, pioneered by Seymour Papert. Constructionism posits that while learners create mental models to help them learn, creating a meaningful product actually strengthens their learning. Seeing that product or the process of creating the product reveal a concept reinforces the student's understanding of that concept. These ideas are also prevalent in the experiential learning model, which espouses learning by doing. Experiential learning involves not just an interactive, hands-on component, but a period of reflection and analysis about what was experienced (*Wikipedia*, 2017a).

This type of learning is very much a part of maker activities. The driving force of most maker projects is a desire to solve one or more problems while creating an object. It seems like a natural fit to devise maker activities that teach or reinforce lessons for students to learn.

"What we're seeing is a resurgence in experiential learning," says Jim Hirsch, former associate superintendent for academic and technological services at Plano ISD in Texas. "Campus leaders have the confidence to go back to learning that's better connected to the way brains work" (Rix, 2014).

"Today's makerspaces are firmly in the 21st century," says Eric Sheninger, principal of New Jersey's New Milford High School. "It is a mash-up of differentiated learning experiences combining traditional elements supported by new technologies. Much more responsibility is given to students in the modern makerspace for their own learning than in the past, when activities were much more teacher driven" (Rix, 2014).

The Drive for STEM Experiences

For several years, there has been an interest expressed in education to increase content and study of science, technology, engineering, and mathematics, otherwise known as STEM. Whether tied to increasing national competitiveness, filling open positions in high-technology fields, or broadening the intellectual capacities of students, the need for increased STEM learning opportunities has been a focus of educational efforts. While there is some discussion on whether there is really a gap or lack of STEM-ready graduates to fill needed positions, increased education in these areas does not appear to have a downside. Finding ways to connect students with existing makerspaces or finding opportunities to add maker activities into the curriculum (perhaps into libraries) will help increase STEM exposure. See figure 2.2 for a STEM learning program.

There is a related drive not only to improve students' abilities in science and mathematics but also to involve the arts in this process. Adding the word *arts* to STEM creates something called STEAM, which adds acronym exposure to the performing and visual arts. The idea is that students gain skills from music, art, dance, and other arts complementary to those built within the traditionally linked science and math. The arts are thought to be effective in holdings students' attention while aiding in the development of their cognitive skills, and adding this type of creative variety can actually improve scientific pursuits. This approach is even more fitting to the breadth of creativity available in many makerspaces, where engineering and artistic creations can exist side by side and also as integrated efforts. As Colegrove summarizes, "Rather than isolated in monastic study, 'almost all Nobel laureates in the sciences are actively engaged in the arts as adults.' Perhaps surprisingly, rather than being rewarded by an ever-increasing focus and hyper-specialization, genius in the sciences seems tied to individuals' activity in the arts and

Figure 2.2.   Army supports STEM and Beyond Night. *Image provided through a CC BY 2.0 License by U.S. Army RDECOM, http://www.flickr.com/photos/rdecom/8518139625.*

crafts." He also notes that famed American inventors Robert Fulton (steamship) and Samuel Morse (telegraph) were both artists before becoming inventors (Colegrove, 2017: 7; Colegrove quotes from an article that appeared in the *Journal of Psychology of Science and Technology*, which can be found at https://www.researchgate.net/publication/247857346_ Arts_Foster_Scientific_Success_Avocations_of_Nobel_National_Academy_Royal_So- ciety_and_Sigma_Xi_Members).

⊚ Making as It Can Be

What can we look forward to in the future of making? While it may be many years still before we have replicators capable of instantaneously creating objects out of subatomic particles as seen on *Star Trek*, the growth of affordable computer-driven sewing and cut- ting machines alongside 3D printers and scanners points toward a much more flexible and open world of making. Putting high-quality creation tools in the hands of a wider group of people could lead to greater variety in products, whether made for individuals or leading to the creation of new smaller brands in several industries. Open-source sharing of designs can make it easier for new makers to get into the market. Beyond designs, a number of maker equipment companies and projects such as Adafruit, Arduino, and RepRap have chosen to operate under open patents in order to keep plans for their equipment available to the community, even if bought out by a larger company (*Wiki- pedia*, 2017c). Will this lead to a more diversified marketplace composed of many small makers competing with large manufacturers across the web? That is the potential of the maker movement.

⊚ The Maker Mind-Set and Libraries: Why Do This?

So, how did librarians become involved in making? In an informal 2017 survey of librar- ians who either have or are planning to have a makerspace (see the appendix for details), respondents were asked, "When people ask you why you have a makerspace, what do you tell them?" Here is how a few of them responded:

- "To allow students hands-on learning opportunities and to have exposure to new technologies that allow them to be creative, tinker, and learn from failure."
- "Libraries are here to democratize access to resources. Historically that has just been books and journal articles. Then it included computers and Internet access. Now it includes making resources!"
- "It's a way to let kids figure things out on their own. It's real. It's problem-solving. It's individualized."
- "It is an opportunity for students to take risks and learn from failure in a consequence-free environment. It is also a place in which students have the op- portunity to participate in activities and experience technology they won't interact with in the classroom."
- "The library is a central location on campus accessible to everyone, regardless of status (student, staff, faculty, etc.) or discipline. Part of the job of the 21st century library is educating people about new literacies. A makerspace is a logical way to advance both the democratic and educational goals of the library."

- "Just as a library democratizes access to books and computers, we also want to democratize access to high-tech machines that would otherwise be unattainable for regular people. Also we stress the library as a community gathering/cross-pollination site and encourage makers to mingle and learn from each other."
- "A library has always been a place to think, dream, and imagine. We have books, and so much more."
- "Makerspaces provide a place for collaboration, critical thinking, troubleshooting, determination, education, and innovation. We spark interest in hobbyists and help hone skills to close our local jobs gap."
- "To facilitate collaborative learning and tinkering, in order to build 21st century skills. Also to provide access to tools and materials that our community wouldn't otherwise have."

These librarians, along with many others, are opening up their libraries to makerspaces. They recognize that libraries are now partnering with their communities in the production process by providing the tools of production along with instruction on its use. "The maker culture has found a new home in our libraries. We need makers and they need us" (Bronkar, 2017: 4). They are effectively broadening their mind-sets to include the creation of items because of these essential points:

- Making is in keeping with the library's mission to provide access to resources and technologies.
- The library is already a makerspace, based on the activities going on within the library.
- The library gives community members a place to come together and support one another's creations.
- The library can support educational efforts in STEM and other areas through hosting a makerspace.

These statements can be turned into questions for any library: Do these points fit your library setting? Could they if you reexamined your library's role? Continue reading to see how libraries have begun implementing makerspaces.

⊚ Library Makerspace Profile: The Collaboratory, Hillsboro Public Library, Hillsboro, OR

http://www.hillsboro-oregon.gov/collaboratory

Janelle Youngblood, Strategic Initiatives Library Assistant, Hillsboro Public Library

How Did Your Makerspace Come to Be?

The Collaboratory grew out of the Hillsboro Public Library's Library of Things, (www.hillsboro-oregon.gov/libraryofthings), which offers kitchenware, technology equipment, musical instruments, and household equipment among other items, and a desire to continue to provide alternative library services in support of the library's mission of encouraging the pursuit of lifelong learning. As the Hillsboro Public Library's strategic plan provides for programming and services to serve the community's interest in lifelong learning, including arts, crafts, and technology, the Collaboratory is intended to reflect patron interest, and to provide access and opportunity for patrons to explore making in an intentionally social space.

The Collaboratory was also inspired by weekly maker labs designed and facilitated by Youngblood's colleague at the Hillsboro Public Library, library assistant—and all-around STEM guru—Deepa Chandra. The weekly labs, geared toward families with young children, featured paper circuitry, 3D printing, basic microcontroller programming, and arts and crafts projects. The popularity of these labs and their strong tie-in to the library's strategic plan energized the Collaboratory development process.

Work on the Collaboratory began in earnest with a community assessment. Youngblood surveyed library staff and patrons, inviting them to complete an online survey, answer prompts on a whiteboard located in a high-traffic area in the library, and use window markers to write and draw on the Collaboratory's fish-bowl windows while the makerspace was under construction. Youngblood asked what *makerspace* meant to patrons, what tools patrons would like to use, and what types of events patrons would like to attend. Patrons and staff were also invited to contact Youngblood directly with specific questions or concerns. Youngblood determined that patrons and staff were enthusiastic about a makerspace; that their interest in tools and equipment aligned with the interest demonstrated by the circulation statistics of the items in the Library of Things and attendance at STEM and arts-and-crafts-focused events; and that patrons were interested in attending both formal classes and open lab-type events. Patrons and staff also expressed interest in health and safety concerns, as well as target audiences and funding sources.

Figure 2.3. The Collaboratory at the Hillsboro Public Library's Brookwood location offers art, craft, and technology tools to patrons in an intentionally social environment.

An underutilized computer lab was converted to house the Collaboratory at the Brookwood Library. The computers in the space were redeployed elsewhere in the library, and the existing tables and chairs were repurposed for the Collaboratory. The original equipment inventory and event proposals, as well as the physical arrangement of the makerspace, were prepared by Hillsboro's "librarian of things," Brendan Lax. Even as Youngblood undertook responsibility for the development of the makerspace, Lax, in his role overseeing the Library of Things, remained an essential support and consultant for the project. Other city administrative, facilities, and technology support staff were vital to the purchasing, installation, and maintenance of the equipment in the Collaboratory.

Who Uses It?

The Collaboratory is open to everyone ages ten and up, and a library card is not required to use the space. Local industries provide an especially rich pool of technology professionals and their families who are frequent users of—and volunteers in—the Collaboratory. Educators and their families, as well as local homeschooling groups, are also frequent users and volunteers.

The Collaboratory is staffed for classes, open labs, and meet-ups. Everyone is welcome to attend these events, regardless of skill level. Classes in the Collaboratory offer instruction in quilting, crochet, Arduino, paper crafting, 3D printing, inquiry-based learning, and serging among other topics; open labs are free time for people to come in and make something with others; and meet-ups are opportunities for like-minded makers, for example, microcontroller enthusiasts, paper crafters, and knitters, to get together and share ideas and skills.

When the Collaboratory is unstaffed, it is available for self-serve use by certified users. To become certified, users must attend a training session and demonstrate they can use the tools in the space properly and safely. Once a user is certified, he or she is given a key code to access the Collaboratory during unstaffed self-serve time.

This mix of use options (self-serve, open lab, meet-ups, and classes) allows the resources of the Collaboratory to be available all of the hours the library is open with no additional staff. Continuous access was a key priority of Collaboratory service.

How Do You Market the Makerspace?

Youngblood works with the library's public information staff and social media team to market the Collaboratory inside the library and around the community, and the Collaboratory itself is also branded with the library's logos and imagery. Youngblood and her colleagues also promote the Collaboratory at community events, distributing flyers and bookmarks advertising upcoming events and offerings.

Who Supports It?

The Collaboratory is generously funded by the Friends of the Hillsboro Library.

What Does It Include?

On opening in the spring of 2017, the Collaboratory contained 3D printers, digital and manual die cutters, sewing machines, a serger, knitting and crochet supplies, paper and fabric cutting tools, an iron and ironing board, building and modeling kits, a stop-motion video kit, a DSLR (digital single-lens reflex) camera, a light box, a green screen, Arduino 101s and components, Intel Edisons and components, a Snap Circuits kit, drawing tablets, a mat cutter, art supplies and crafting materials, and laptop computers.

How Do You Stay Aware of Developments in Makerspaces?

Youngblood networks with local maker librarians and monitors the YOUmedia Community of Practice, as well as popular technology blogs and vlogs. She also regularly browses commercial offerings by library and STEM vendors. Youngblood reports that word of mouth and personal recommendations have also been enormously helpful in targeting local interests and capturing experiential knowledge. Youngblood also toured several local not-for-profit makerspaces to network with other maker professionals and generate ideas for the Collaboratory.

What Do You See Happening in Your Makerspace in the Next Year?

Youngblood hopes to see patron involvement continue to affirm and direct the Collaboratory's offerings as it develops. Specifically, she hopes to expand digital media software and computing potential, and offer additional fabrication tools such as laser cutters and CNC (computer numerical control) mills. With help from her technical support staff, Youngblood plans to continue working toward an untethered one-to-one computing model, where each user could use a Collaboratory laptop to "plug and play" with any of the tools and equipment in the space.

In addition, Youngblood would like to offer presentations and workshops highlighting STEM education efforts and design thinking methods. She would also like to see increased awareness of and involvement with the project in the community.

What Is Your Advice to Others Who Would Like to Create a Makerspace?

Youngblood advises a phased model to others who would like to create a makerspace. This model, as opposed to creating a makerspace with the support of a large grant or funding source, allows for adjustment of the space, equipment, and programming. In a public library especially, it is essential to demonstrate concrete interest in and the value of new library service areas. Following a phased model provides ample opportunities to assess patron interest, address maintenance issues, and incrementally alter service models.

Youngblood has also built flexibility and planning into the project's service and staffing model to allow for smooth schedule changes and adaptive strategic goals. For example, in addition to an online calendar of events, the Collaboratory posts a "What's happening now" sign in the window to encourage flexibility and serendipity among users. And while the Collaboratory relies heavily on volunteers to staff open labs and meet-ups, Youngblood attempts to schedule events so that she or a proxy could step in as necessary. This flexible and adaptive attitude also goes a long way toward successfully aligning Collaboratory events and services with the library's strategic goals.

⊚ Library Makerspace Profile: The MILL, University of Idaho Library, Moscow, ID

http://mill.lib.uidaho.edu

Kristin Henrich, Head, User and Research Services, University of Idaho Library

How Did Your Makerspace Come to Be?

The idea for the Making, Innovating, Learning Laboratory (MILL) first developed during planning for a library first floor renovation in fall 2015. Library administration supported the creation of a makerspace within the library and thought that locating such a space on the first floor would serve as a high-visibility illustration of their dedication to providing accessible, interdisciplinary technology spaces for teaching and learning. Library faculty convened a task force in December 2016 to discuss early considerations of philosophy and logistics, and planning took place over several months. The project quickly coalesced, and the MILL was open for student use on the first day of fall semester, August 22, 2016, nine months after planning began.

Who Uses It?

Created with the goal of providing centralized, open access to innovative technology across disciplines, the MILL is open to all university-affiliated students, staff, and faculty. Several campus departments have dedicated 3D printers and other maker technology, but access is limited to students within those disciplines and there are often barriers to use that prevent open exploration. The MILL promotes an environment of inclusive peer learning, provides open and equitable access to technology, and facilitates a low-risk creative space where students can explore. The most represented disciplines for drop-in visits are virtual technology and design, mechanical engineering, and art and architecture; they have also taught discipline-specific workshops for chemistry and art, and have worked with faculty in anthropology, biology, and business to incorporate 3D printing into assignments. In addition to curricular work, the MILL also offers an average of thirty-two workshops per semester, highlighting various skills or technologies; popular offerings have included "Dissect a Laptop," "Screen Printing via Vinyl Cutter," "Intro to SketchUp," and "Button Making 101." These workshops are a good draw for staff and faculty looking for lunchtime distractions and serve to promote and market the space as well as provide instruction.

How Do You Market the Makerspace?

The MILL has an active social media presence, with accounts on Facebook and Instagram. Events such as workshops are cross-promoted on both of these platforms, and student work is highlighted as often as possible. First-year experience librarians promote the space and the resources in their library instruction sessions with introductory courses, and the MILL is a popular stop on building tours. Staff are in the process of developing a branded print marketing strategy, and have had success inviting the school newspaper to various workshops and events. The MILL is also dedicated to supporting underrepresented populations in STEM, and targets outreach to groups such as the Society of Women Engineers, the Office of Multicultural Affairs, and the Native American Student Center.

Who Supports It?

The MILL is financially supported by library funding and is directed by Kristin Henrich, the library's head of user and research services. A joint project between the User and Research Services department and the Data and Digital Services department, the MILL is a collaborative effort that relies on library faculty and staff enthusiasm and knowledge to offer dynamic content. The MILL is open twenty hours a week and is staffed primarily by student workers with some oversight by permanent library staff. The popularity of the lab, and the opportunities for integration across the curriculum, are prompting the development of a permanent, full-time position to manage the space and daily operations, which will be filled by fall 2017.

What Does It Include?

The MILL values both analog and digital making, and the equipment and resources available in the space supports that commitment. The MILL offers a typewriter, sewing machine, button maker, and origami and other paper crafts, as well as more wired technology. This technology includes two 3D printers, a 3D scanner, a vinyl cutter, the Adobe Creative Suite, Makey, Arduino, Raspberry Pi, and more. The MILL is also finalizing plans for the Studio, a dedicated audiovisual production and editing space. This space, located on the second floor of the library, includes a green screen, lights, microphones, and video cameras, as well as audio and video editing software.

How Do You Stay Aware of Developments in Makerspaces?

Henrich says that subscribing to LibraryMakerspace-L out of the University of Florida has been incredibly helpful, both for seeing trends and connecting with other makers. She also suggests joining up with a state or regional maker cohort as another good way to keep abreast of what peers are doing, and seeing what is or isn't relevant for the target audience. It's easy to get caught up in the "next big thing" in makerspaces, so it's nice to have a group of fellow librarians who are also involved with makerspaces to bounce ideas off of. Twitter can be great for this, too—find some other makers and follow them, or join in a #MakerChat!

What Do You See Happening in Your Makerspace in the Next Year?

The MILL is hoping to become more formally integrated into the curriculum, and in partnership with faculty, develop purpose-built assignments around making technology. The library will also be developing a formal assessment program, refining some of its existing assessment tools and examining information gathering practices. As of summer 2017, the library will be hiring a dedicated staff person to serve as MILL manager, and will be opening the Studio to students, staff, and faculty.

What Is Your Advice to Others Who Would Like to Create a Makerspace?

There is an abundance of information about makerspaces in the literature and online; makers are a prolific and inclusive bunch! This can be great, but it can also be distracting and discouraging when getting started. You are the expert on your community and your patrons; start with what your students have asked for, and determine what needs they have that aren't being met. Identify what resources might meet those needs, and then go to the literature to research technical details and best practices. If possible, visit other makerspaces in your area; it is vital to develop a cohort that you can consult later in the development process, and seeing an existing space up and running can inform how you visualize what you'd like your space to look like. You can do it!

⊚ Key Points

- Making is a constant but evolving human endeavor.
- The maker movement arose to combine digital tools and open-source sharing to create physical and digital objects.
- Makerspaces can affect education by increasing exposure to STEM and STEAM concepts and activities.

⊚ References

Bronkar, Cherie. 2017. "How to Start a Library Makerspace." In *The Makerspace Librarian's Sourcebook*, edited by Ellyssa Kroski, 3–28. Chicago: American Library Association.

Colegrove, Tod. 2017. "Editorial Board Thoughts: Arts into Science, Technology, Engineering, and Mathematics—STEAM, Creative Abrasion, and the Opportunity in Libraries Today." *Information Technology and Libraries* 36 (1): 4–10.

Costello, Laura, Meredith Powers, and Dana Haugh. 2017. "Pedagogy and Prototyping in Library Makerspaces." In *The Makerspace Librarian's Sourcebook*, edited by Ellyssa Kroski, 29–36. Chicago: American Library Association.

Rix, Kate. 2014. "Meet the Makers." *Scholastic Administrator*. http://www.scholastic.com/browse/article.jsp?id=3758299.

Wikipedia. 2017a. S.v. "Experiential Learning." https://en.wikipedia.org/wiki/Experiential_learning.

———. 2017b. S.v. "Maker Faire." https://en.wikipedia.org/wiki/Maker_Faire.

———. 2017c. S.v. "Open Source Hardware." https://en.wikipedia.org/wiki/Open-source_hardware.

———. 2017d. S.v. "Participatory Culture." https://en.wikipedia.org/wiki/Participatory_culture.

CHAPTER 3

An Overview of Makerspace Implementations

HOW CAN LIBRARIANS BRING THIS TYPE of maker culture and mind-set into their libraries? What are other libraries already doing in order to create these spaces, equip them with the tools that enable making, and develop maker programming and activities? How can libraries invigorate and infuse their missions to include modern making? As this chapter demonstrates, there are many ways to get started creating a new makerspace.

To get a sense of what makerspaces in libraries look like, an informal survey was conducted in 2017 that had 273 respondents (see the appendix for details). Of that total, 219 librarians responded affirmatively: 164 respondents (60 percent) said they have a makerspace or similar space in place and 55 (20 percent) said they plan to add a makerspace. The other 54 librarians responded that they did not have a makerspace nor did they plan to add one; those responses eliminated them from being included in the questions that followed.

Makerspaces appear in most types of libraries: ninety-four (43 percent) of the respondents are in public libraries, seventy-four (34 percent) in academic libraries, and forty-two (22 percent) in school libraries. The remaining two (1 percent) are in special libraries, while none selected the option of "other" libraries.

Library makerspaces are found throughout the United States and around the world and are overwhelmingly recent additions to their libraries. Libraries in forty-four US states and four other countries (Australia, Egypt, Ireland, and the United Kingdom) responded to the survey. In terms of their makerspaces' longevity, fifty-nine respondents (27 percent) noted that their makerspaces had been in place for one to two years, fifty-seven (26 percent) for less than one year, thirty-four (16 percent) for two to three years, sixteen (7 percent) for three to four years, and thirteen (6 percent) for more than four years. Librarians who had not yet implemented a makerspace made up forty (18 percent) of the responses with "other" as their response.

Naming a makerspace was an interesting process for the librarians who responded. From the survey, 170 of the 219 makerspaces (78 percent) have been named in some way or are located in existing digital creation spaces with their own names. The term *makerspace* was incredibly popular in the names, with 63 named spaces clearly identified as a makerspace. Other spaces had these popular terms somewhere in their names:

1. Lab (27)
2. Maker (14)
3. Creative or creation (14)
4. Studio (8)
5. Digital (7)
6. Library (6)
7. Media (6)
8. Innovation (4)
9. STEM or STEAM (3)
10. Idea (3)

So, one approach might be to combine several of these words for a clearly top-of-the-line makerspace. For instance, the Library Digital Media Creation Maker Lab Studio has a nice ring to it, doesn't it? Seriously, though, it is interesting to see the use percentage to learn how makerspaces are being positioned in the communities in which they exist. Also, it is good to know that *makerspace* is a recognizable enough term to name a space after, while it is clear that other variations seem to work well, too. A word cloud showing the repetition of terms used in the names is included in figure 3.1.

Figure 3.1. What's your name? Terms used to describe makerspaces.

◎ Starting Your Makerspace

Cherie Bronkar (2017) suggests following these ten steps to start a library makerspace from scratch.

1. Determine your makerspace focus: Consider your demographics and budget to determine what will fit your library's needs. Will it be a technology-focused space or one that focuses on arts and crafts, or will it be a digital media space?
2. Establish funding: Research grants and funding sources (covered in the next chapter) to supply your makerspace with needed equipment and materials.
3. Get started without funding: Consider starting off with maker activities that can be achieved on a shoestring budget, through donations, or else consider hosting "bring your own supplies" events.
4. Evaluate your space design: Consider equipment placement, ventilation, supplies storage, noise levels, number of electrical outlets, data ports, and so on as you plan. Take measurements and make diagrams.
5. Get started with equipment lists: Bronkar presents several starter lists of equipment ranging from $500 to $50,000 depending on makerspace focus; for example, technology focused, media focused, and so on. There is also a helpful list of more than one hundred products on Makerspace.com (2016). Additionally, the Daring Librarian (2015) has a $350 Makerspace Starter Kit List available.
6. Identify new roles: Prepare staff for new roles as makerspace facilitators through professional development training.
7. Determine expectations: Set expectations for staff who will be hired or selected to fill the roles in the new makerspace.
8. Construct a training plan: Training librarians for your new makerspace can be achieved by bringing in vendors to train on specific equipment or by visiting other libraries with makerspaces to learn from their librarians.
9. Identify and arrange professional development: Seek out Maker Faires and local maker events and meetings to allow your staff to continue to develop their skill sets.

10. Establish policy: Determine what will be allowed within your makerspace, including what will be made. Set age, training, and usage limitations in your policy, and consider costs when deciding if you will charge fees for materials or equipment use.

Forming Your Makerspace

Libraries might use other approaches beyond Bronkar's ten steps. The following allow alternative entry points that might work better for some libraries.

Recognize the Makerspace within Your Library

This is not as simplistic a suggestion as it might first appear. You cannot simply call a library a makerspace and then it becomes so. But you can look at your library with new eyes and identify existing activities, services, and technologies that are already providing making experiences for library patrons. For instance, your academic library might check out microphones and cameras to students for video projects. Or your school library computers might be used by students to play Minecraft after their required assignments are completed. Or your public library might host knitting groups or have craft sessions as part of its summer reading program. These are maker activities, and while they may not be all that you want to offer or everything that your community would like to make in the library, they do provide you with some maker cred: a foundation for what could be. You can recognize that you have a makerspace already and declare that your library is one.

The Slow Build

Jump into the creation of a makerspace, but do not add everything right away. There is no set of required services, technologies, or operations that you must have to get started—no top ten list to check off or you can't use the name. Add something—either in response to the wishes expressed by your library users or to spark some creativity and get people thinking—then you can build from there. And there should be no reluctance to move into maker mode, given the potentially positive impact that it can have on your community.

Start Big

The direct opposite of the slow build is to build a space that will accommodate many types of making at once. Having enough funding to do so is essential to make this happen, but it also requires a different mind-set from the more gradual nature of some of the earlier approaches. Starting off with a dedicated space and a lot of equipment is a way to stay ahead of ongoing demands for new capacities from your makers and to encourage interplay to happen among different making technologies. It is setting off with the expectation that you will have multiple making projects going on simultaneously. You might choose to do this because your goals for a makerspace are bigger than just introducing a few maker activities. Perhaps you are also trying to meet various kinds of maker needs, from engineering students creating prototypes of products to people experimenting with Arduino kits and groups taking photography classes. At 20,000 square feet, the University of Oklahoma's sprawling Innovation Hub makerspace (profiled in chapter 8), has a budget of $4 million. That is far bigger than what most makerspaces will ever be, but it provides an upper end of the scale of building big. If you hope to inspire your community with your makerspace, starting big will introduce many opportunities at once and can lead to cross-pollination of creativity. Again, the money and a concrete plan have to be in place to pull this off (more on these considerations in chapters 4 and 5).

Do It by the Book

An approach that can work as a stand-alone method or in cooperation with the other approaches is to find a model makerspace that you would like to emulate, see what it has, and follow its plan (either entirely or in part). This could work with a model that is either a large space or a small space. The draw of this approach is that you are avoiding re-creating the wheel and are outfitting your space in a manner that works. You are starting with a design that may have taken the other makerspace years to build and, in doing so, saving yourself that time. A caution with this approach is to not merely try to replicate the model space but to adapt it to fit your community's needs and interests. A couple resources that can be helpful to use as plans or that point to sample plans are the *Youth Makerspace Playbook* (Maker Ed, 2015), and Maker Media's *Makerspace Playbook* (2013). You may also glean insight into how to create a library makerspace from the experience of twenty plus librarians in the book *The Makerspace Librarian's Sourcebook* (Kroski, 2017).

Engaging Your Community

Regardless of the approach, it is essential to keep your community in mind. The most incredible library makerspace is not a creation unto itself; it needs to reflect the interests of the library's community. Suggestions on gauging and building interest come in chapter 4, but it is crucial to understand that if makerspaces are all about making, there have to be makers who come to the space. An underutilized room of expensive equipment is not the outcome that you are looking for as you follow these approaches. You will want to begin by doing your best to encourage a maker culture among library staff as they will be the ones facilitating many of these activities and supporting and troubleshooting the equipment when it gets finicky. Gaining librarian buy-in for these spaces is critical to their ongoing support and sustainability. The second and even more important task is to see where a makerspace can serve the community.

Creating Interest versus Overwhelming

A word of guidance regarding makerspaces is that they be neither too large nor too small. While this sounds like most of Polonius's equivocating advice to his son Laertes in Shakespeare's *Hamlet* ("Neither a borrower nor a lender be"), there is a useful lesson here. The goal of the library makerspace is to meet existing community needs for creative experiences while trying to motivate the rest of the community to create. Imagine your community as populating a dartboard. Those in the bull's-eye are the people you have solidly in mind as you are planning your space and who are (hopefully) giving input on the planning. As you move further out in the rings of the board, each border that you cross is populated by people who will need higher amounts of convincing that the makerspace is for them.

While you may never interest people at the farther reaches, you have to find the right balance of offerings to keep the committed group interested and returning while not scaring off potential users. Now, what might scare them off? It could be that your makerspace has too much high-tech equipment and looks like it is a place for engineers only. Your space could have just a couple of items to start with and not encourage people to inquire for more, or your makerspace might be too focused on artistic creation, for instance, and not attract someone who might be interested in robotics. Not every makerspace is going to serve the entire community of the library, nor is every makerspace trying to reach the most reluctant members of the community. But as you are trying to get started and create interest, you should have the preponderance of your offerings match what you know will be used, but you should still have something on hand that will make people curious and draw them in (e.g., a 3D printer, soldering irons, examples of completed projects).

⑥ Programming versus Open Labs

While planning a makerspace, be sure to specify the following: will the library provide dedicated space to use for maker activities or instead offer programming on maker technologies and topics? Or will it offer both? This may be a question that changes over the lifetime of your makerspace. You might hold occasional workshops or a monthly series of programs to start off your efforts and then move to offering open hours in a makerspace in the library. Or your library setting might not lend itself to holding public programs and instead might find making activities linked to specific class needs. Perhaps that would evolve into open, creative periods with your maker activities. Yet another possibility is that your maker operations are always mobile, moving from site to site in your community, without opening an actual space. This is a consideration that should definitely go into the planning for the space. Chapter 11 discusses programming ideas and ways to balance these two approaches.

⑥ Getting Dirty in Your Making

Although there are multiple forms and requirements for various makerspaces, one element is a concern for all: clean versus dirty spaces. Many maker activities are relatively clean: computer programming, sewing, LEGO robotics, green screen videography, even most 3D printing. They probably will not threaten most library furnishings or carpet with damage or stains. Yet, soldering, woodworking, computerized numerical control cutting machines, cooking, and ceramics might make a mess. They might also smell bad, make a lot of noise, or create fumes that need to be vented out of the building. It is crucial for the impact of the making to be considered—both on those in the makerspace and on patrons in the rest of the library. This includes the annoyance factor as well as safety considerations. The environment available in the library may guide the choices of making that can occur there. At the very least, you have to imagine what the makerspace will look like if everything you envisage happening there is actually going on. If dirty space is not available or cannot be planned for in the initial launch of the space, it can always be added in later.

⊚ Considering Different Library Types

More approaches or issues may arise depending on your library's setting. While many maker activities will be mostly identical in implementation regardless of the setting, particular areas of focus can come into play. Separating these library types out briefly should not overshadow the potential for multitype library partnership efforts for making either.

Public Libraries

Can public libraries continue to carry on their mission of providing information access to the public by adding access to creative equipment? They can, and actually some argue that public libraries are on the forefront of the makerspace movement (Bronkar, 2017). Otherwise, many members of the public might not have access to fabrication equipment. Public libraries have the broadest population to reach and can target makerspace activities to specific groups and the community at large. Teens' and children's activities can be the focus of a defined makerspace area or mobile maker programming. Adults can also have opportunities to create. Patrons may wish to create artwork, learn how to design products, or collaborate on efforts that lead to small businesses. Here is another opportunity for the multiplying impact of the public library's purchases to be felt in the community: the library makes the purchase, and several individuals and organizations can benefit. Libraries can market to many possible groups, and depending on the interest shown by the community, it can be difficult to meet everyone's needs.

Academic Libraries

On college and university campuses, makerspaces may be the realm of engineering, design, and science students practicing the talents that they will apply in an industry upon graduation. They may also be aimed at a wider audience of students working on projects, from creating prosthetics for animals to brain scans turned into 3D puzzles (Bronkar, 2017). The academic environment provides many opportunities for maker equipment and activities to have a direct tie to learning. One question that might occur is why teaching and research departments do not just add their own makerspaces. Some may have them already, but these spaces tend to not match the number of hours that the library can be open. This is often a capacity of the academic library that makes it a perfect place for the makerspace.

School Libraries

School library makerspaces are generally geared toward adding hands-on interaction to the school setting and pursuing STEM initiatives. The school day and curricular demands are tight on time, and maker activities are often added only when they clearly add to students' potential for learning. There are many making activities that can meet this criterion, and that makes the makerspace a viable component for schools and school libraries. It is also possible, once a makerspace is equipped in the school library, to use open periods and after-school times to let students stay engaged inventing, creating, and building their skills.

ⓖ Library Makerspace Profile: Makerspace at Lawrence University
Seeley G. Mudd Library, Appleton, WI

http://blogs.lawrence.edu/makerspace

Angela M. Vanden Elzen, Reference and Web Services Librarian and Assistant Professor, Lawrence University Seeley G. Mudd Library

How Did Your Makerspace Come to Be?

A group of about twenty faculty and staff at Lawrence University came together over a desire to increase the availability of 3D printing for their students. The chemistry department had a 3D printer for many years, but it was getting old and it could not be easily accessed by non-chemistry students. This interested group of faculty and staff held meetings and discussed ways the 3D printers could be used in their courses and work, as well as additional tools and equipment they'd like to have available for their students. This information was put into a grant proposal that was submitted to the Associated Colleges of the Midwest, an organization of which Lawrence University is a part.

In regard to the location, everyone on the planning committee agreed that the library would be the ideal location for this space. The library has long hours, is frequented by students from all academic backgrounds, and happened to have an underutilized space that could double as a makerspace.

Who Uses It?

When the makerspace was first constructed, the target audience was faculty who would then use the space with their students for coursework. While this does still occur, the makerspace is now largely used by students for a variety of reasons. Some students have come up with creative ways to integrate makerspace equipment to complete an assignment or senior capstone or honors project; other students want to learn more about new technologies in hopes that it will make them more marketable in graduate school or the workplace; and other students have asked to learn about 3D printing and design through in-depth independent studies and tutorials. It is also used frequently by students in the newly formed makerspace club.

How Do You Market the Makerspace?

The library markets the makerspace through social media, namely, Instagram, Twitter, and Flickr. Library staff do their best to follow student organizations and campus departments and post targeted content. The makerspace is also marketed through events that Angela M. Vanden Elzen and her staff host, such as open houses, guest speakers, and summer coffeehouse presentations.

Who Supports It?

As part of a grant, the library received funds to obtain the major equipment, and to cover enough consumables to get the space up and running for the first year. Ongoing costs have been covered by the library media center budget and the information technology

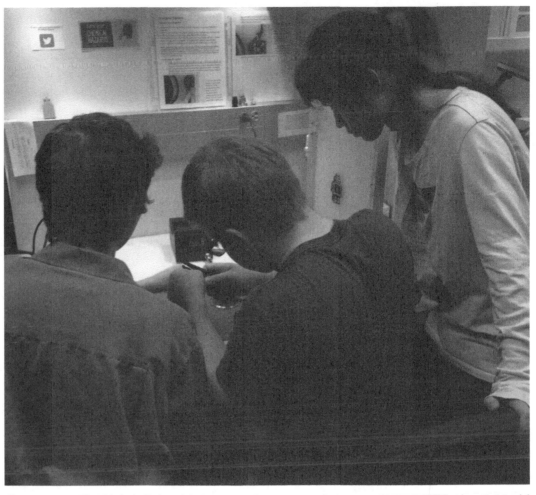

Figure 3.2. The Maker Club soldering at makerspace at Lawrence University Seeley G. Mudd Library. *Photo courtesy of Angela M. Vanden Elzen, Lawrence University.*

services department. Many department chairs have offered to contribute to the ongoing costs when classes from their departments use the space for a required assignment, but that has not been necessary as of yet. As the makerspace club grows, they will request a student club budget and contribute their own consumables, supplies, and equipment.

What Does It Include?

The makerspace includes the following:

- 3D printers: Ultimaker 2+ and Ultimaker 2+ Extended
- 3D scanners: Matter and Form desktop 3D scanner and Fuel3D handheld scanner
- Sewing station: Singer Sew Mate 5400 sewing machine and many sewing supplies
- Electronic cutter: Silhouette Cameo
- Painting and collage supplies

How Do You Stay Aware of Developments in Makerspaces?

- E-mail newsletters from 3D object repositories like Sketchfab, Thingiverse, and MyMiniFactory are extremely helpful in keeping up with trends in 3D printing.

- The library has a subscription to *Make:* magazine. This magazine covers a wide array of maker projects and includes very helpful product reviews.
- Social media is a great way to keep updated with trends in makerspace. Makerspace interest groups on Facebook, such as MakerSpaces and the Participatory Library, are helpful, as is following other library and nonlibrary makerspaces. A lot of interesting tips and projects can be learned by following hardware and software Facebook pages, such as Autodesk's Tinkercad, Ultimaker, Silhouette America, and Glowforge. The trend of auto-play videos on Facebook provides an excellent opportunity to quickly discern the challenge and safety level of a project. Instagram is another great social media application that lends itself well to sharing final products and short videos of projects in progress.
- Attending sessions at professional conferences is also a good way to not only learn about developments, but also make helpful connections with colleagues who share an interest in makerspaces.

What Do You See Happening in Your Makerspace in the Next Year?

After multiple requests for a standard laser cutter—which will not work for the Lawrence University space for safety and ventilation reasons—Elzen and her staff are hoping to get a Glowforge. While still a laser cutter, the Glowforge has been designed for use in interior spaces with little ventilation and comes with an air filter. It is also much more affordable than a standard laser cutter and claims to be more user-friendly. The release date has been moved back a few times for this much-anticipated product, but the staff hope to have one within the next year. They also hope the student makerspace club will become more established and gain a larger awareness on campus.

What Is Your Advice to Others Who Would Like to Create a Makerspace?

- Establish roles ahead of time. Be sure that everyone involved with overseeing, training, ordering, and so on knows what's expected of them at the formation of the makerspace.
- Organize the space well from the start. Going back to organize is difficult when you're trying to work with patrons at the same time.
- Gather and compile usage statistics from the beginning to get a good idea of how often your space and equipment are being used, and to have evidence for when you want to add more equipment and tools. It can be time-consuming to go back and compile a year's worth of statistics when the administration requests statistics.
- Organize your time so that you can continue to keep up on the advancements in software and hardware upgrades, and to improve your skills. Don't only spend time in the makerspace doing troubleshooting.

ⓖ Library Makerspace Profile: SPE_MakerSpace, Speegleville Elementary School, Waco, TX

https://www.facebook.com/SpeeglevilleElementaryLibrary

Christe Hancock, Teacher Librarian, Speegleville Elementary School

How Did Your Makerspace Come to Be?

Speegleville Elementary is an innovative campus. When Christe Hancock first learned of Maker Faire and MAKE spaces, she knew it had to happen in her school library. School libraries, after all, are the largest learning spaces on most campuses. The spaces lend themselves well to makerspaces, and there is also usually a very well-educated media specialist who knows how to help students find things and do things. First, Hancock wrote and received a $5,000 foundation grant from her district. Then she gutted the out-of-date research section of the library where she is teacher librarian. The makerspace was the first of its kind in the school district and has been visited as an example by other school districts, campuses in the district, the local university museum, the newspaper, television, and National Public Radio.

Who Uses It?

The makerspace has been first used by enrichment classes every day. These students are chosen from the GT program and the top tier of RtI. Teachers have begun sending kids to work in the space for project-based learning and checking out the materials to use in their classrooms. Maker Mondays allow kids to come before school starts to work in centers that have been requested.

How Do You Market the Makerspace?

SPE_MakerSpace makes itself known through social media (several Facebook pages, Twitter, and Instagram) faculty meetings, and school board meetings.

Who Supports It?

SPE_MakerSpace is supplemented by many budgets: library, book fair, gifted and talented, and PTA.

What Does It Include?

The space houses desktop computers, a 3D printer, 3D pens, sewing machines, circuits, gears, Chromebooks, LEGOs, robotics, woodworking, and crafts. It has moveable furniture and whiteboards, both regular and interactive. The campus is 1:1 iPads, so iPads are used *daily* not only in the integration of what happens in the space but also in documenting, collaborating, and sharing. Coding and project-based learning figure heavily in what happens in the space, including Bloxels.

How Do You Stay Aware of Developments in Makerspaces?

Hancock follows many listservs that specifically speak to the school library makerspace. Texas has two great conferences, which she attends—TLA (Texas Library Association) and TCEA (Texas Computer Education Association)—and which are at the pulse of all things makerspace, sharing information for funding, materials, lessons, and all the latest amazing things "out there." She also attends every Maker Faire that comes close to her for ideas and motivation.

What Do You See Happening in Your Makerspace in the Next Year?

Hancock sees more student and teacher participation and using the space in spectacular ways, and more flexible use of the library/makerspace areas. She sees the evolution of teachers' ideas of makerspace, more goodies, and more student interaction in what is provided in the makerspace.

What Is Your Advice to Others Who Would Like to Create a Makerspace?

Speegleville was lucky enough to start with a good amount of money, but if your library hasn't, don't let that keep you from doing a makerspace! Find the room and start adding to it. Start with low-tech: duct tape, origami, puzzles, recycled materials, games—whatever you can lay your hands on that will get kids interested in using their minds and their hands. Enroll with NAIER.com to get materials for a great price. Put out the word about what you are doing. Make a wish list on paper and with Amazon.com. Build it and they will come!

Key Points

There are makerspaces in nearly all types of libraries in the United States and the world. There are multiple ways to approach implementing a makerspace in your library. Some key points to remember from the chapter follow:

- Making sure that the library is in tune with its community is essential to the success of the makerspace.
- Several considerations can guide librarians to find the right fit for the makerspace, including the types of programming and the types of making that will go on there.
- Public, academic, and school libraries will have specific considerations to consider when creating a makerspace.

The next chapter examines the many options available for maker technologies and making activities.

References

Bronkar, Cherie. 2017. "How to Start a Library Makerspace." In *The Makerspace Librarian's Sourcebook*, edited by Ellyssa Kroski, 3–28. Chicago: American Library Association.

Daring Librarian. 2015. "Makerspace Starter Kit." June 6. http://www.thedaringlibrarian.com/2015/06/makerspace-starter-kit.html.

Kroski, Ellyssa. 2017. *The Makerspace Librarian's Sourcebook*. Chicago: American Library Association.

Maker Ed. 2015. *Youth Makerspace Playbook*. Maker Education Initiative. http://makered.org/wp-content/uploads/2015/09/Youth-Makerspace-Playbook_FINAL.pdf.

Maker Media. 2013. *Makerspace Playbook, School Edition*. http://makerspace.com/wp-content/uploads/2013/02/MakerspacePlaybook-Feb2013.pdf.

Makerspaces.com. 2016. "Makerspace Materials." https://www.makerspaces.com/wp-content/uploads/2016/11/Makerspace-Materials-Supply-List.pdf.

CHAPTER 4

What Will Patrons Make in Your Makerspace?

IN THIS CHAPTER

▷ Learning What Other Library Makerspaces Are Making

▷ Evaluating the Most Used Items in the Survey Makerspaces

▷ Assessing What Makerspaces Still Need

▷ Choosing Making Options: Results from the Survey

▷ Making Decisions about Making in Your Library

▷ Satisfying Your Community

▷ Library Makerspace Profile: Science and Technology Makerspace, Mill Park Library, Victoria, Australia

▷ Library Makerspace Profile: The Fab Lab, Dyer Elementary School, South Portland, ME

LIBRARY MAKERSPACES ARE COMPRISED of a vast array of different maker tools and technologies ranging from 3D printers to robotics kits to arts and crafts supplies. No single library makerspace can hope to include all of the endless possibilities, but instead may strive to provide inspiration and access to the tools and equipment that are most desired by its particular communities. By looking at what types of technologies and activities other library makerspaces include along with actual patron interests, librarians will be able to better determine the focus and direction of their own emerging spaces.

To begin the discussion of makerspace options, take a look at the results of the survey of library makerspaces (see the appendix for details). Although it is not an all-inclusive list of every type of making included in libraries, it is a good first step in the process of imagining opportunities to offer patrons in your library. A short list of the most common maker technologies and activities is included in chapter 1, but the complete list of options is listed in table 4.1. Of the list of fifty-five items, all but three were selected by at

Table 4.1.   Technologies and Activities in Library Makerspaces (n = 219)

TECHNOLOGY/ACTIVITY	RESPONDENTS	
	%	N
Computer workstations	66.7	146
3D printing	65.8	144
Arts and crafts	64.8	142
Computer programming/software	48.4	106
3D modeling	46.6	102
Photo editing	45.2	99
Video editing	43.4	95
Tinkering	43.4	95
Arduino/Raspberry Pi	41.6	91
Robotics	36.5	80
Scanning photos to digital	33.8	74
Other (please specify)	33.3	73
Electronics	30.1	66
Fabric shop (sewing machines, leather sewing machines, CNC embroidery machines, etc.)	28.8	63
Vinyl cutting	25.6	56
Soldering iron	24.7	54
Animation	23.3	51
Digital music recording	22.8	50
Creating a website or online portfolio	22.4	49
High-quality scanner	22.4	49
Prototyping	19.6	43
Soft circuits	19.6	43
Game creation	18.3	40
Inventing	16.9	37
Circuit hacking	16.0	35

TECHNOLOGY/ACTIVITY	RESPONDENTS	
	%	N
VHS conversion equipment	13.7	30
Electronic music programming	12.3	27
Laser cutting	11.9	26
Electronic book production	9.6	21
Digital scrapbooking	9.1	20
Large format printer	9.1	20
Computerized numerical control (CNC) machines	9.1	20
Creating apps	8.2	18
Woodworking (table saw, panel saw, bandsaw, drill press, etc.)	5.9	13
Food/culinary arts	5.5	12
Mobile development	4.6	10
Jewelry making (acetylene torch, buffing station, annealing pans, forming tools, etc.)	4.6	10
Plastics/composites	4.6	10
Milling machine	4.1	9
Screen printing	3.7	8
Industrial sewing machine	3.7	8
Silk screening	1.8	4
Bicycle building/maintenance	1.4	3
Ceramics	1.4	3
Mold making	0.9	2
Potter's wheel and kiln	0.9	2
Letterpress	0.9	2
Stained glass	0.9	2
Welding	0.9	2
Dark room	0.5	1
Blacksmithing	0.5	1
Metal shop (metal lathe, cold saw, horizontal bandsaw, sheet metal, etc.)	0.5	1
Automotive	0.0	0
Guitar repair	0.0	0
Glass shop (glass blowing, kiln, jewelry making, etc.)	0.0	0

least one makerspace (those three were glass shop activities, guitar repair, and automotive activities). The items included in the list were gathered from surveys conducted to help create new library makerspaces and from technologies and activities mentioned in the makerspace literature.

⑥ Other Technologies and Activities in Library Makerspaces

3D pens	Makey Makey kits
Adult coloring	Microscopes
Button makers	Mobile kitchen
Chemistry sets	Origami
Coding tools	Papercraft
Die-cut station	Puzzles
Duct tape crafts	Shrinky Dinks and plastic art
Google Cardboard	Recording studio
Green screen and video production	Snap Circuits
Knitting and crocheting	Stage with sound and light boards and digital output
Laminators	
Leatherworking	Telescope and GPS astronomy tools
LEGOs	Virtual reality programs and headsets
littleBits	Weaving looms

Another aspect to consider from the survey results is the number of technologies in use at each makerspace. From the 219 library makerspaces represented in the survey, respondents chose technologies or activities from the list of fifty-five a total of 2,168 times. That means that the average makerspace in the survey is offering nearly ten making options to its patrons. A few respondents listed only one technology or activity, but the majority had a list of items in the double digits. This would suggest that for most library makerspaces, making is not a one-trick operation; the libraries have chosen to include multiple making methods for their patrons to explore.

To make the list a bit more complete, the responses that composed the "other" category on the survey are shown in the textbox. Additional technologies were added in seventy-three responses. They bring a bit more specificity to some of the survey options (e.g., Sphero, Google Cardboard, or littleBits) and add interesting applications not included in table 4.1. For instance, having a presentation space with a stage is an intriguing addition to a library, as is a weaving loom or astronomy equipment. Some other listed items likely should have made it onto the original survey from the start, such as the button maker, LEGOs, and video production equipment.

Again, even with the others added, the list surely does not reflect everything that is going on in library makerspaces, especially since it reflects the offerings of only 219 makerspaces. Taken together, the lists do provide you with approximately eighty-two options for your makerspace. The remainder of the book, particularly chapters 6 through 10, will identify other options as well. Recognizing a sampling of the universe of options to include in your makerspace can help you prepare to make choices.

⊚ Evaluating the Most Used Items in the Survey Makerspaces

Going further, you can find direction on what is actually being used in existing library makerspaces. In addition to the many examples from the literature that this book references, an additional question in the survey asked respondents to list the items or technologies that get the most use in their makerspaces. Nearly 170 respondents answered the question, with all but a couple of them offering multiple technologies that are used the most. The most common response was 3D printers with almost one hundred makerspaces finding that technology was one of the most used. Table 4.2 illustrates the top fifteen most popular tools, technologies, and activities in today's makerspaces.

While respondents included many digital technologies in their selections, more classic options appeared, such as heat guns, glue guns, and coloring pages. And it's interesting that arts and crafts activities rival computer stations and audiovisual production equipment. There were also interesting combinations of most-used items, such as "arts and crafts and coding/computer technology" or "long arm quilting machine, 3D printer, laser

Table 4.2. The Top Fifteen Most Used Technologies and Activities

TECHNOLOGIES AND ACTIVITIES	N
3D printers	97
Arts and Crafts	22
Computer workstations	21
Legos	18
Audio/visual equipment video/sound production equipment	17
Laser cutter	17
Robotics	11
Snap Circuits	10
Sewing machines	10
Button maker	9
VR	7
Coding	6
Vinyl cutter	6
3D pens	3
3D scanner	2

cutter, and robotics." The patrons who use these makerspaces have varied interests and are perhaps not afraid to jump from more physical to more digital activities. The ethos of collaboration among makers of different forms can thrive in a coworking environment where multiple technologies and activities are supported.

◎ Assessing What Makerspaces Still Need

The final question in the survey asked respondents to discuss what they hoped to add to their makerspaces in the next year. One hundred sixty-four respondents with makerspaces already in place responded. The choices that recurred the most included a 3D printer/3D modeling/3D scanner (forty), sewing machines and fabric arts (twenty-one), and virtual reality equipment (twelve). Table 4.3 represents the twelve most sought-after tools and technologies for makerspaces within the next year.

Table 4.3. Top Twelve Wish List Items for Next Year

WISH LIST ITEM	N
3D printer/3D modeling/3D scanner	40
Sewing machines and fabric arts	21
Virtual reality equipment	12
More space	11
Robotics	10
Legos	10
Laser cutter	10
Workshops and classes	9
CNC machines	7
Video and audio production equipment	6
Coding	6
More staff	4

◎ Choosing Making Options: Results from the Survey

In the same survey, respondents were asked how they decided which technologies they should offer in their makerspaces. They were guided to choose all options that applied to their makerspaces. The most popular response was "modeled on other makerspaces," chosen by 134 librarians (61 percent). This is certainly a popular technique for many physical and virtual changes in libraries, where tours, written accounts, and visits to websites can influence the development. Next came "suggestions from patrons" with 94 responses (43 percent) and "input from educators" with 89 responses (41 percent). The choice of "donations of equipment," with 59 responses (27 percent), reflects an interest from members of the community that goes further than mere words. As with any donation in a library, the equipment may be a welcome addition or something unexpected and not immediately useful. And finally, "patron surveys" came back with 30 responses (14 percent). Looking to those who will use or guide the use of the makerspace seems like a logical method. And finally, there was also an "other" category with 71 responses (33 percent), which is likely made up of a variation on one of the earlier choices or a "not applicable" choice for those makerspaces still in the early planning stages.

Making Decisions about Making in Your Library

As you gather input and information on designing your makerspace, look to the methods described here as a guide. The following section examines these methods in detail and suggests ways to use the inputs of data, options for making, and perhaps donated items to build a space that can positively affect a library's community.

Remember that making can take many forms. As the survey indicated, arts and crafts endeavors exist in nearly as many libraries as do 3D printing activities, so not all makerspace pursuits involve cutting-edge technology or even computers. The world of choices for making awaits!

Find Other Examples in Libraries

So how do you locate other library makerspaces? As with many finding tasks, a little Googling will get you started (e.g., "makerspaces libraries public"). What is quite helpful to this task is the fact that so many library makerspaces are out there. More than a few have now been chronicled at length in the library literature, including in the previous edition of this book —for example, Anythink Brighton in Colorado, Allen County Public Library in Indiana, and Bibliotheekservice Fryslan in the Netherlands; many others have been written up in local news sources and will likely appear in library publications over time. The bibliography can point you toward many profiles of library makerspaces. Also, the eighteen library makerspaces that are profiled in this book provide you with examples to learn from and individuals to contact for more information. A growing web resource is MakerBridge (http://makerbridge.si.umich.edu), which provides a forum for library makerspaces to share their questions and their presence. Additionally, the Facebook group MakerSpaces and the Participatory Library boasts over 4,560 members.

There is a danger inherent in finding model library makerspaces in that you will be moved to duplicate their offerings and services without further consideration. That could lead to an easy process of matching equipment purchases and copying program ideas, without enough attention paid to one's own community. The greater value in this research and the conversations that might occur is to see what is working for another library (ideally, several other libraries), to talk with the staff to see how they made their choices, and then to apply this process in your own environment. The examples of other libraries can provide assistance in comparing competing products, testing the efficacy of programming methods, and lending clues to developing the activity in another community. These experiences also let you envision making it work in another library setting.

Find Other Makerspaces in Your Community

Another route to take is to locate a makerspace in your community. This opportunity can provide you advice from those with expertise in making equipment and processes, as well as gaining insights on programming and perhaps gaining a partner or source of volunteers for your own making effort. Here are some methods for finding makerspaces:

- Makerspace.com has a directory of makerspaces at http://makerspace.com/makerspace-directory.
- The *Make:* magazine site has a list of maker community groups at http://makezine.com/maker-community-groups.
- The MakerMap (themakermap.com) is an open-source directory of making organizations and sites that provides a browsable and searchable Google Maps interface to help you locate local and regional makers.
- Similar sources include Hackerspaces (https://wiki.hackerspaces.org/List_of_Hacker_Spaces) and MIT's Fab Lab List (fab.cba.mit.edu/about/labs).

Local makers can give you insights into what types of making are already going on in your community or region. That might open up complementary making opportunities for you to hold in the library, or it could point out unmet interests or needs that you could take on. Visiting a makerspace could provide excellent how-to information for your library makerspace development, and joining one can give you hands-on experience with products and machines before you buy them yourself. The spirit that moves libraries to share making technologies can benefit you as you make plans and develop funding for your space.

Consider Staff Talents

As many library makers have discovered, their own colleagues can help guide the direction of a makerspace through the input of their talents and interests. You might have no idea that someone on your staff is a woodworker, or can program Arduinos, or has a talent with crafts away from the job. They might be interested in teaching others how to do that activity, even if that might not be their regular role at the library. You might be inspired by the staff talents that you find, to pursue making options that match those talents and to even seek to alter staff roles to help bring a makerspace into fruition. Finding capable individuals to help patron makers and to help guide the development of a space can be a challenge, but do not forget to ask around as you begin thinking about a makerspace. Doing so can lead to some interesting opportunities, even if it is someone taking on an occasional workshop or covering a few hours of time assisting patrons in an open makerspace environment. And if there are individuals on staff who know a bit more about 3D printing or soldering than you do, they can help you plot out the realities of working with that technology.

Be Inspired by Makers

While this can go hand in hand with visiting local makerspaces or talking with talented staff members, opportunities to watch or read about makers at work can provide ideas for making to add to your library. Recommended sources are located everywhere, from craft fairs to local businesses. You could have some interesting conversations with a maker that might lead to someone teaching a session at your library.

Each of the flagship Maker Faires in New York, Chicago, and the Bay Area have a section of their website called "Meet the Makers" featuring hundreds of inspirational makers, which can be viewed in a slideshow or browsed by category. Discover motivating makers through these fantastic directories, such as Acme Muffineering, a group of really smart folks who build cupcake and muffin cars; Benjamin Hylak, an award-winning maker and acclaimed roboticist; or Code Hobbits, a group of middle school and high school students who have built a smart umbrella, sound-reactive headphones, a mood-reactive world map, and more (Maker Faire, 2017).

Consider Other Partners

Beyond local makers, there may be other organizations in your community that you could connect with and find a mutual making activity or partnership. The engineering club on your campus might have a 3D printer but lack the space to keep it running. There might be local crafters who would love the opportunity to gather in your library and would be happy to have more individuals join their group. Science teachers or a robotics team in the local schools might support and use the STEM-based educational opportunities that your school or public library makerspace provides. As you begin looking around your community, think about what might interest a potential partner in working with you in a making activity, and talk about your thoughts whenever the opportunity arises. There may be common ground available in places and with groups you never considered.

Gathering Input from Patrons and Other Interested Parties

As you shape your makerspace plans, you should consider not only the views and interests of established groups but also those of the individuals you hope will use the makerspace. Surveys are a great method for marketing your eventual makerspace (it lets people know that you are adding something new) and for gauging your community's interest in specific making activities. You can easily create simple web surveys using Google Docs or SurveyMonkey, and you will find many examples of past surveys by Googling "makerspaces survey." You can also print copies of the same survey to capture individuals you might not reach through electronic means. For a combined version of these two approaches, you could also have a web survey in your browser on a tablet that you encourage library visitors to fill out. Apart from individual surveys, you can use whiteboards or flip pads on easels to gather ideas from individuals who might not have time to fill out a full survey but who could respond quickly to a single question. The *Makerspace Playbook* includes sample surveys for potential makers and for those who might be interested in mentoring in your makerspace (Maker Media, 2013).

Seek Donations

No makerspace would want to limit its program to what can be supplied by donors, but why not seek out interested people and groups in your community who might be willing to provide materials? It never hurts to ask and see what local groups or businesses might be able to offer. You want the needs of your makers to define how the space grows in services and activities, but donations from groups and individuals can be a part of that definition process. As you brainstorm donation possibilities, consider these questions:

- Could you work cooperatively with a local makerspace on a Maker Faire and then have the makerspace donate some teaching time at the library?

- Could you make the case that your projects contribute to STEM education and then have a company donate materials toward improving its future workforce?
- Are the projects that you are working on able to turn someone else's trash into your maker's treasures? Companies with scrap materials to dispose of might be willing to pass some of them your way.

Form a list of items that you can really use and would accept from donors. It is a good idea, though, to be realistic about what you can actually use the equipment for and how soon it could be put into use. If someone donates a jet engine for your makerspace, how does that fit into the skills and interests of your makers? Beyond local sources, look at TechSoup.org for technology donations for nonprofit organizations and libraries and DonorsChoose.org for donations to schools.

⑥ Satisfying Your Community

Ultimately, the purpose of the makerspace is to provide the greatest benefit to its makers, so be sure to keep that in mind as you gather input and choose making activities. Remember that the makerspace is not a one-and-done sort of enterprise. You will start off trying to interest people in the types of making that both you and they thought would be great to learn. Some of these types will pan out, and others may fall by the wayside after a time. The makerspace will need to expand its offerings to meet new needs and interests or to reach deeper into one area of knowledge to take makers toward greater expertise.

You will have to stay aware of new developments in making, and chapter 12 offers a variety of means to do so. The initial surveys of your makers cannot be the end of your information gathering either. A regular assessment of patrons' reactions to workshops and open making times will guide your development. Some choices of technologies and activities will be clear-cut, but do not be afraid to take a chance on adding something interesting to your makerspace. The suggestions in this chapter will help you get ideas and start your makerspace moving.

⑥ Library Makerspace Profile: Science and Technology Makerspace, Mill Park Library, Victoria, Australia

Cory Greenwood, Learning Coordinator, Mill Park Library

How Did Your Makerspace Come to Be?

The Science and Technology Makerspace at Mill Park Library was initiated by a former staff member who received a grant to fund a small community project. The library identified an opportunity to ride the wave of the maker movement, which really started to gain momentum across Australia in 2013, and set out to install the first makerspace in a Melbourne public library.

The teenage reading room was redeveloped into the makerspace with new furniture, tools, and resources purchased to activate it as a space for creative experimentation and exposure to new technology. The goal was to provide access to new technologies people couldn't otherwise afford, particularly 3D printing and high-end computer software.

Access was complimented by resources such as Lynda.com and regular programming designed to showcase the technology's potential.

In the years since its inception, the space has evolved to provide regular STEAM focused programs, partnering where possible with local government and community groups to help facilitate learning opportunities. Makerspace programs are starting to be incorporated with traditional library programs; robots appear at preschool story times and augmented reality coloring sheets are occasionally used in place of traditional craft activities at our after-school program.

Sister makerspaces have since been developed across the library's region, each with their own focus or discipline: textile and craft; writing and publishing; design and multimedia.

Who Uses It?

Makerspace programs are predominately attended by school-age children, but programs are developed for people of all ages and abilities. The library facilitates intergenerational learning opportunities on weekends and evenings, pairing children with seniors or encouraging parents to engage with their child's learning.

3D printing services are most often used by students and enthusiasts. The library currently does not charge for this service but reviews all requests on a case-by-case basis.

The space is open for the community to use outside of programming hours; some use it as a meeting or co-working space, others use it as a private study zone. The library takes pride in providing a flexible space that caters to the differing needs of the community.

How Do You Market the Makerspace?

Makerspace programs have unique branding, which helps the Mill Park Library community identify which programs specifically have a STEAM focus. They are advertised alongside the library's literary and cultural events in print and digital collateral. Marketing of the physical space is driven by program advertising and thoroughfare; makerspace resources are taken out of the library and showcased at community festivals, local shopping centers, and community houses.

Who Supports It?

The makerspace is supported by skilled library staff and volunteers from local government and various community groups. The library provides ongoing funding for consumables (3D printing filament, electronics components, craft supplies, etc.) and has a budget for external program facilitators to elevate learning opportunities and upskill library staff.

What Does It Include?

The makerspace focuses on new technologies, piloting a range of multimedia and design-focused programs that can be adapted for other service points and sister makerspaces in the region. It has iPads, 3D printers, a 3D scanner, dedicated Raspberry Pi PC stations, Arduino invention kits with a variety of components for prototyping, littleBits, Makey Makeys, drones, LEGOs, LEGO Mindstorms, a green screen with professional lighting and camera equipment, Adobe Creative Cloud software, and smart TVs.

New benches were installed last year to improve access to power outlets and enable the Raspberry Pi PCs to be permanently set up in the space. Prior to this, monitors, keyboards, and mice would be hauled from a storage area and set up in the middle of the room. This was less than ideal and presented a number of health and safety risks, including tripping hazards with power cables running across the floor. The new configuration allows more users to occupy the space and allows the tables on wheels to be positioned by the community as needed.

How Do You Stay Aware of Developments in Makerspaces?

Library staff subscribe to e-newsletters and network with other professionals via Facebook groups and Twitter. The library subscribes to *Make:* magazine, and a variety of industry publications are circulated amongst key staff. Library staff attend conferences and share their experiences at networking events.

What Do You See Happening in Your Makerspace in the Next Year?

The makerspace will continue its partnership with the local government's sustainability team, building and learning about environmental monitoring systems to check and regulate things like water temperature in an aquaponic system that has been set up in the library.

The library hopes to expand on its electronics program next year to provide soldering equipment and single-use, take-home electronic projects.

NAO, the humanoid robot, is being considered for purchase and will be the focus of a new program tailored to teens.

A scientific discovery club for preschoolers (children aged three to five) is being considered as a potential partnership program with the Children's Discovery Museum in Sydney, Australia.

A gamified games development course tailored for children with autism spectrum disorder has been developed and will have a second run next year.

What Is Your Advice to Others Who Would Like to Create a Makerspace?

Listen to your community and create flexible, collaborative, and inviting spaces that can be used by people of all ages and abilities. Don't buy what they won't use or can already afford; find out what they can't afford and go buy that instead.

Utilize staff interests and expertise but don't be afraid to outsource or partner with other organizations if it means providing a unique opportunity for your community. Upskill whenever possible and learn alongside the community; there's no shame in being a beginner, especially when in the realm of new technology.

⊚ Library Makerspace Profile: The Fab Lab, Dyer Elementary School, South Portland, ME

https://dyerelementary.wordpress.com

Megan Blakemore, Library Information Integrator, Dyer Elementary School

How Did Your Makerspace Come to Be?

The idea was the brainchild of Principal Elizabeth Fowler, who saw the potential in a former computer lab. She had the idea of letting fifth grade students design the space through a project-based learning experience. So, the fifth grade students spent the first part of the school year researching what a makerspace is and determining what belongs in an elementary school makerspace. They created dioramas and wrote persuasive arguments, which they presented to the community, including the school board.

Who Uses It?

Students use the space during recess time ("Tinker Time") and before school as part of an innovation team. They can also use the space and materials as part of the library curriculum and with their classroom teachers.

How Do You Market the Makerspace?

Professional development time is used to generate use and enthusiasm among teachers. Students learn about opportunities through announcements and posters.

Who Supports It?

The principal and the district tech director support the space through professional development, and they also seek out funding. The space has community support through visiting makers, that is, makers who volunteer to share what and how they make with students.

What Does It Include?

Based on student input, the Fab Lab includes a LEGO wall, 3D printer, circuitry tools (littleBits, Snap Circuits), robotics, woodworking, and crafting supplies.

How Do You Stay Aware of Developments in Makerspaces?

Twitter, blogs, and magazine and journal articles keep the staff aware of developments in makerspaces.

What Do You See Happening in Your Makerspace in the Next Year?

Tinker Time has taken a challenge-based approach. In the next year, Megan Blakemore hopes to more closely tie these challenges to the design process so students follow the challenge from problem to brainstorming to designing and building, testing, redesigning, and sharing. Blakemore and Principal Fowler hope to continue to push the maker ethos into the classrooms.

What Is Your Advice to Others Who Would Like to Create a Makerspace?

Start with your patrons. The students and teachers in a school library makerspace are the users of the space, so find out what they want and need, and then build your makerspace around them.

⊚ Key Points

For patrons to start using the library's makerspace, decisions need to be made about which making options to add. Some key points to recall from the chapter follow:

- Existing library makerspaces exhibit a myriad of maker technologies and activities.
- Library staff should use a variety of methods to seek out options for and guidance on making in a proposed makerspace.
- The makerspace must meet the needs and interests of its community.

The next chapter addresses the crucial question of funding to carry a makerspace forward.

⊚ References

Maker Faire. 2017. "Meet the Makers." http://makerfaire.com/bay-area-2017/meet-the-makers/.
Maker Media. 2013. *Makerspace Playbook, School Edition*. http://makerspace.com/wp-content/up-loads/2013/02/MakerspacePlaybook-Feb2013.pdf.

CHAPTER 5

Budgeting for a Makerspace

WHILE THE KNOWLEDGE-sharing aspects of the maker movement are free, the tools and equipment that facilitate making are most certainly not. To this end, librarians must locate new means of support in order to fund their pursuit of developing a makerspace or incorporating maker activities into their library. There are a variety of funding opportunities, some of which are unique to makerspaces, including seeking grants, asking for donations, charging fees for equipment use, and more. This chapter delves into the ins and outs of financially supporting a makerspace, including developing a working budget for not only equipment and supplies but also staffing, furniture, training, and more.

Pricing Your Makerspace

What expenses go into forming and sustaining a library makerspace? It all boils down to what you feel will best serve your community.

Given the range of options and levels of service, a makerspace could conceivably be implemented for a few hundred dollars (e.g., circuitry kits, Raspberry Pi and Arduino kits, craft and sewing supplies, simple tools for tinkering, LEGOs, etc.), or it could run into many thousands or even millions of dollars (e.g., adding multiple 3D printers, scanners, laser cutters, and CNC [computer numerical control] milling machines) (Bronkar, 2017). The Milwaukee Makerspace Wiki (2017a) has an extensive equipment list that includes detailed specifications for each tool, photos, notes, and even manuals and training information. This would be a great place to start browsing; also look at the wish list in order to start your own. As well, there's the "Makerspace Materials" supply list (Makerspaces. com, 2016), which provides more than one hundred products that you might want to start off with. As you create a wish list of items and activities using the methods in chapter 4, you can then turn to your budget and assess what you can really afford. What follows are some cost categories to plan for as you develop your makerspace.

Staffing

Who will support your makerspace activities? Will your current library staff members take on the additional duties as needed, or will they shift some of their time away from lower-priority tasks? Will you identify dedicated staff members to staff the makerspace, or will you spread the responsibility for the space throughout the staff? Will you depend on volunteers you recruit specifically for the makerspace to cover the space's open hours or other programming? Or will you hire new staff to take on the makerspace duties or allow current staff to shift over to this work?

These questions point at issues involving both the nature of the makerspace and the expectations that you have for staff. There is a sliding scale of makerspace activity and availability that needs to be decided on before you can assess staffing, and the examples given in chapter 3 can help you make these decisions. Your makerspace may not be a set place in the library but rather mobile equipment that is used both inside the library and in various outreach locations in your community. You may have only monthly makerspace programs in place or a limited set of times when the space is available for open use by patrons. Once you figure out how often and in what form your makerspace will be available, you can address the amount of staffing that those activities will require.

Chapter 11 covers methods for offering makerspace services and ways to consider making use of staff and volunteer time. The key takeaway from this section is that personnel costs have the potential to be the highest ongoing input into your costs. Starting to sketch out your needs now is essential.

Equipment

For questions about equipment, chapter 4 is the place to go for further discussion of how to identify options to include in the makerspace. Once you have a list of activities and equipment in hand, you should price out the bigger-ticket items, from CNC routers to video-editing stations and from 3D scanners to green screens. You can then move along to more affordable items, estimating the numbers that you will need of each. A great strategy is the idea of starting with a wish list that can be assessed for costs and then winnowed down to essentials. While a wish list can be mindful of other budget considerations, such as limitations of space or staffing, it can also be used as a long-term, modifiable planning document. You might add and price technologies that you are not sure you are ready to accommodate, with the idea that if they are too expensive or too involved to implement right away, you can keep them in mind for later additions. The main thing here is to not forget to settle on some technologies and to get their acquisition costs down on your budget.

Space Addition and Renovation

Perhaps a given library makerspace will not use space in the library, or it might fit into already existing spaces (e.g., a meeting or group study room, a newly opened-up corner of the reference area following the removal of shelving). If this is your library, you may be able to skip this section of the budget. But if your makerspace plan involves designating a separate space and putting up walls or making a substantial change to an existing space, even adding carpet, then you will have some costs to add to the budget. You might be so fortunate to be able to piggyback on another project for the library, school, or campus, in which case your makerspace area can be attached to a larger project to build an addition or an entire new branch or other facility. This can help you collaborate in the previously planned larger change and not have all the costs associated with your makerspace.

More often, though, the makerspace is being developed within an existing structure, with some options for renovation or some additional walls. In addition to these more involved renovations, it is good to consider whether the area will need more electrical outlets or network drops to accommodate the equipment you are adding. Be sure to walk out the space and think of anything that would help the makerspace work really well there. As with the equipment wish list, you may identify changes for the next time around or once additional funding is available after the makerspace is well established in the library.

Furniture

Now that you have considered what the area of the makerspace will look like, who will be working there, and what stuff will go into it, you need something for people to make upon. It may be that you already have furniture to repurpose from other areas of the library or the area that you are converting into the makerspace: computer furniture, tables, chairs, and whatnot. But if you are adding new technologies and you lack pieces of furniture to set them on, this should go into your thinking. Rolling carts and other contrivances to hold equipment or materials for a more mobile makerspace experience could be included in this category. Chapters 6 through 10 note any specific furniture needs that the kinds of making profiled in those chapters might require. The key here is to make your makerspace comfortable and functional for people to create in.

Consumables

Remember the paper! It is all well and good to budget for a top-of-the-line multifunction device for your printing and copying needs, but do not overlook the multiple reams and sizes of paper that you will need to buy over the months and years to use it. Many making activities cannot be completed without consumable items such as paint, plastic, wire, and paper. Do not forget to work a cost estimate for these refillable materials in your budget. Chapters 6 through 10 have sections that remind you about consumable items that you will need to have on hand and regularly replace for your making activities. The *Makerspace Playbook* (Maker Media, 2013: 75, 77) also has two lists of consumable items that can be helpful for coming up with your own list.

Training

Very clear decisions will need to be made on who is responsible for learning, teaching, and guiding the making in your makerspace. No one may need to be the jack-of-all-trades with skills from origami to soldering to 3D design, but you need to determine who on your staff will have a central role in planning and running the space. It can be a single coordinating individual or a team approach. Making skills may already be present among your staff members, but even in the best-case scenarios, you will need to allow for time to hold training sessions and for staff members to try out equipment and other technologies to achieve a level of comfort. Beyond training library staff members, you will need to think about who will teach patrons to work with the makerspace materials. Again, you may have interested and skilled individuals on the staff, but you may also need to reach out to volunteers or paid instructors. The Milwaukee Makerspace Wiki (2017b) has an excellent collection of training checklists detailing important points about machines and equipment you're likely to find in a makerspace, such as laser cutters, CNC milling machines, drill presses, table saws, and so on.

The survey of library makerspaces found that they most often had library staff members teach classes (176 responses, or 80 percent of all responses). Volunteers (51 responses, or 23 percent) and paid instructors from beyond the library (37 responses, or 17 percent) were the other two most common choices for teaching classes, with 50 respondents (23 percent) choosing the "other" category, which likely represented the 55 libraries that are still in the planning stage of their makerspace.

Outreach and Events

Some of your operating costs will also involve expenses associated with holding workshops, mobile events, or mini Maker Faires. Aside from the already covered overhead items of space, staff, equipment, and furniture, you may have to increase the amount of consumables that you would need to accommodate workshop participants. You might also need to budget for additional marketing, transportation, and giveaway costs for these events. If you are committing to offering making in your library or through your library programs, you need to invest in the process.

ⓖ Crafting a Budget

While going through the potential expenses of your makerspace, it is necessary to start creating your budget. Be as realistic as possible in deciding on figures for the items in your budget. The research that you have completed on product choices and other libraries' implementations will help you fill in the budget lines. Additional resources for you to consult are included in chapter 12. At times, you will need to estimate amounts for situations where you cannot find an exact model for your planned service or where firm figures are unavailable. You may find it useful to plot out your items on a document like the library makerspace budget worksheet shown in table 5.1.

Sample budgets or equipment lists may also be useful guides and indicate additional expenses that you had not yet considered. The *Makerspace Playbook* (Maker Media, 2013: 61) has a sample budget that shows some equipment and item costs; it also has a graduated cost perspective depending on how much money a library has available and what

Table 5.1. Library Makerspace Budgeting Worksheet

CATEGORY	ITEM DESCRIPTION	NUMBER OF ITEMS	COST PER ITEM	TOTAL COST
Staffing				
Library staff time				
Paid instructors				
Equipment				
Must-haves				
Could-uses				
Maybe-somedays				
Furniture				
Consumables				
Training				
Staff training expenses				
Paid instructors				
Outreach and Events Costs				
Marketing				
Additional consumables				
Transportation				

additional items can then be added. Jeri Hurd, a teacher librarian who launched a library makerspace at the Western Academy of Beijing, shared her equipment list at http://www.scribd.com/doc/179096661/makerspace-equipment-pdf. You should also read through the library makerspace profiles located throughout this book for additional stories of finances and budgeting for makerspaces in libraries.

Financing a Makerspace

Now that you've decided on your makerspace, what are the funding options? The choices available will mirror many of the funding choices available to libraries for any new program or service. Some of the main differences exist in specific grants or donation opportunities, which are detailed here. The first place to look for confirmation of useful methods for makerspace funding is in the results from the library makerspace survey.

Results from the Survey

The 2017 survey of library makerspaces asked respondents to indicate one or more of their sources of funding to start their makerspaces (sources shown in figure 5.1). Of the respondents, 118 (54 percent) said that funding came from the library budget, while 89 (41 percent) reported that they received money from grants, 78 (36 percent) received donations to start their makerspaces, and 35 (16 percent) requested additional funding from their parent organizations (colleges and universities, school districts, city or county governments, etc.). Another 18 (8 percent) chose the "other" category, including 12 makerspaces that were yet unfunded. A total of 338 choices were spread out among the 219 respondents, indicating that each library makerspace averaged approximately 1.54 funding sources.

Making Your Case

So how do you convince others that you need a makerspace? Before jumping into the available sources for funding, a common requirement for seeking any type of funding is the ability to articulate what you need the funds for and why this might be a good idea. Earlier chapters in the book discuss reasons to form a makerspace and can certainly be returned to for arguments to buttress your own reasoning. You need to be able to summarize what you hope the space will accomplish for the potential makers who will use it. As well, you should tie the goals for the makerspace in with the mission of the library and the larger educational goals of your organization. Sharona Ginsberg discusses the need to build a library or school-wide maker culture through internal promotion in order to sustain buy-in and interest in the makerspace. She provides many tips for how to keep up momentum once the space has launched as well, such as building partnerships with local organizations, creating a badging system for patrons to earn as they learn skills, working with instructors to incorporate makerspace activities into their curriculum, and more (Ginsberg, 2017).

The library makerspace survey included a question for respondents to express how they explain to others why they added a makerspace. Examples from their statements are shown in the textbox.

These statements and the word cloud of terms taken from the responses to that question (figure 5.2) can help you build your own explanation of your space. That explanation can then be modified to create grant proposal statements or elevator speech–length expressions, depending on your audience and purpose.

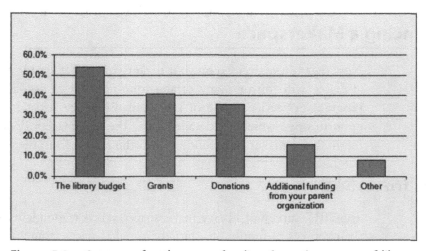

Figure 5.1. Sources of makerspace funding from the survey of library makerspaces.

⊚ Why Libraries Added a Makerspace

- "To help community members have a space to express themselves, and to create a space to have kids learn and grow."
- "Lifelong learning is an integral part of our mission, so we now offer a space where patrons can learn with and from others."
- "Because we believe that learning doesn't just come from reading; it comes from doing. And because we believe that we are helping people develop skills that aren't available anywhere else in our community."
- "It allows students an opportunity to explore and tinker. Students can play games, create circuits, experiment with the pet tornadoes, and more, and while they're tinkering or creating things, they're learning."
- "It's important to have a creative space for making and digital learning so that everyone has access to opportunities to develop their skills and have fun. Digital skills are becoming ever more important, particularly for young people who may not traditionally visit the library. The maker ethos empowers people to become creators rather than consumers."
- "It's a place for students to create, be innovative, learn, invent, collaborate, and have fun!"
- "Making activities provide people the tools and opportunity to learn new skills and work in a collaborative environment."
- "We are providing a hands-on learning and creating environment which is interdisciplinary. Here students can learn about and use tools and processes which they might not encounter in their major."
- "This is an opportunity for people to create, explore, and experiment."
- "To support assignments, to aid students in creating models and replicas, and to promote STEM learning on campus."
- "To create a three-dimensional learning space for cross discipline collaboration. We hope to enhance and supplement the classroom curriculum."
- "It supports our mission statement, which states that we support 'informational, educational, and recreational interests' of our community. Lifelong learning is our goal."
- "Our values include experiential education, partnerships, and collaborative creations."
- "It's a place for tinkering, inventing, and trying new things."
- "Our makerspace is a place for creative learning, becoming digitally literate, and has equipment available to allow creative makers to learn through play!"

Finding Space in the Library Budget

Every library is different, and every library budget is different. That being said, every library can find some money to start up a makerspace, given that the entry point for a makerspace can be fairly low. Money for new initiatives is rarely just lying around, and it tends to come at a subtle shifting of priorities from one area of service toward another and perhaps in a competitive process among various new ideas that the library staff are

Figure 5.2. Words used by survey respondents to describe their reasons for having a maker-space.

considering. Libraries may be able to set aside funding from one year to carry into the next and use the combined funds to start a makerspace. There may be end-of-fiscal-year money available that must be spent quickly, and makerspace proponents should have their justification ready to offer up when the time is right. Not every budget or spending process will allow or encourage these activities, and not every budget will have flexibilities in budget lines that allow a reduction in book spending or database subscriptions to be used for starting a makerspace.

Library staff and administrators need to ask themselves whether they find the creation of a makerspace a priority for their institution: if not, then funding will have to wait for a change in priorities or for external funding to spark internal interest; if so, then they will seek where fluidities exist within the library budget that might free up a few hundred dollars here or a thousand dollars there that could be used to try out a makerspace. Perhaps a small investment in some Arduinos for a workshop or the hosting of a class or two provided by members of a local makerspace could serve as a meaningful trial balloon for future developments. Staff interest cannot be the sole driving force for the makerspace nor its sole funding source. But if the case can be made well to library administration, a small amount of money can usually be found.

Additional Organizational Funding

In some environments, there may be the opportunity for the library to seek additional onetime funds from its parent organization, which might be a college or university, a city, or a school district. It is definitely worth exploring if such funding is an option in your setting. This may be a defined process in that organization, or it may be completely new ground. A carefully explained proposal for funding that has a clear benefit to that larger organization could help you locate funds that will simply be impossible to gain from other sources.

Finding Grants

There are a number of grant programs in place that could be pursued as possibilities for funding makerspaces. These include federal and state government programs, as well as grants from within library organizations, parent organizations such as schools and institutions of higher education, and local and national foundations. Talk with your local development staff or your state library for suggestions on possible funding sources. Some options to consider include an ongoing program of grants for learning labs for libraries and museums from the Institute of Museum and Library Services (IMLS) and the MacArthur Foundation (http://www.imls.gov/about/learning_labs.aspx). Federal grants funded by the Library Services and Technology Act and administered by state libraries may also provide opportunities for makerspace programs (see links to individual state libraries on the IMLS site at https://www.imls.gov/grants/grants-state/state-profiles). Some state libraries have offered specific funding programs to begin making, including New Jersey (http://librarylinknj.org/projects/makerspaces) and Idaho (http://libraries.idaho.gov/page/make-it-library-where-idaho-makers-meet).

Survey respondents were asked to share the specifics of their funding sources and many did so: 114 people mentioned particular sources that they found to finance their makerspace. Table 5.2 indicates the top grant and donation sources received by library makerspaces. And the textbox has a listing of all of the other funding sources that libraries mentioned in the survey.

Table 5.2.   Top Fifteen Donation Sources for Library Makerspaces

DONATION SOURCES	N
Friends of the Library	11
Patron donations	11
Self-funded	8
Local/district education foundation	7
PTA	6
LSTA Grant	6
IMLS Grant	6
DonorsChoose.org	4
Idaho STEM Action Center	3
Staff donations	3
The Library Foundation	2
YEI Project	2
European Social Fund	2
State grant program	2
National Library of Medicine grant	2

⊚ Other Sources of Grants and Donations for Library Makerspaces

Alabama Digital Humanities Grant
Allstate Foundation
ALSC (Association for Library Services to Children) Curiosity Creates grant
Ann Sherry Foundation
Arts Council Grant
The Associated Colleges of the Midwest Faculty Career Enhancement Grant
Best Buy Community Grant
Boise Education Foundation Grant
CCC Makerspace Grant
Central Texas Library System Grant
Clay Electric Round-Up grant program
Community Foundation for Palm Beach and Martin Counties
Community Trust Foundation Grant
Connecticut State Library Grant
Durham Foundation Grant
General Electric
Green Bay Packers Community Foundation
Hancher Foundation
The InfyMakers Grant
Knights Foundation
Kohler Foundation
Laura H. Moore Cunningham Foundation
Local community grants
Local councilors community grants fund
Local humanitarian fair
Local thrift stores
Lowe's Educators Grant
Lowe's stores
McElroy Trust
Mead Public Library Foundation
Mott Foundation
The National Writing Project Grant
OCLC (Online Computer Library Center)
Pacific Library Partnership Innovation Grant
Perloff Family Foundation (local to Maine)
Protect Next Generation State of Illinois
PTO (Parent Teacher Organization) Grant
Reading Olympics
Scholastic Dollars
State Farm
State Library Partnership
Stewarts Shops
Student donations

Fund-Raising and Seeking Donations

Donations of equipment, materials, and time are addressed in chapter 4, but there is also the potential for funds to be donated to your makerspace effort. Crowdfunding opportunities are widely used for funding a variety of maker-led product launches and could also work for libraries interested in starting a makerspace.

In the crowdfunding model, people interested in seeing a product produced or a project funded each contribute a small amount toward the total funding goal. Oftentimes there are rewards offered to those who contribute such as branded swag like T-shirts, postcards, stickers, and so on. Once the creator has met the funding goal, he or she can then produce the item and supply it to those who committed the money (Ginsberg, 2017). Services such as Kickstarter (http://www.kickstarter.com), Indiegogo (http://www.indiegogo.com), GoFundMe (http://www.gofundme.com), and DonorsChoose (https://www.donorschoose.org) exist to manage the funding process, accepting funds from those who are interested in the project, and ensuring that the goals are met.

Libraries could set goals for the equipment needed to start a makerspace and could offer making opportunities to those who fund that equipment. DonorsChoose is a crowdfunding website that is set up specifically for teachers to fund projects happening in their classroom, and GoFundMe is a fundraising website for charities. One innovative high school librarian who has funded many makerspace projects using crowdsourcing is Colleen Graves from Denton, Texas, who has used DonorsChoose multiple times to raise money to purchase supplies and equipment for her students. See figure 5.3 for one of her crowdfunding project banners. And you can view all of her funded projects here: https://www.donorschoose.org/gravescolleen.

Charging Fees

As a whole, libraries are committed to providing access to expensive items of all kinds without expecting any payment from their patrons or perhaps just negligible amounts.

Creative Digital Media and Audio Engineering Station

My students need a Go Pro camera and accessories for making their own movies, Blue microphone for recording podcasts, and midi controllers for our digital media creation workstation, along with instructional books and instrument accessories.

Mrs. Graves
Billy Ryan High School
Denton, TX
Grades 9-12
High Poverty

Figure 5.3. An example of library makerspace crowdsourcing.

They are not money-making ventures and are not generally focused on cost recovery. It is common for makerspaces run by companies or membership organizations to charge monthly or hourly fees for using equipment and to charge for supplies. Libraries running makerspaces need to at least consider a charging structure to make the budgets for their spaces work out.

In the survey of library makerspaces, ninety-nine respondents indicated that they do charge patrons for using the makerspace. That group makes up 45 percent of the total number of respondents who completed the survey. The most common method for charging patrons is to charge for consumables used in the making, with seventy-six respondents (77 percent of those who charge) reporting such a charge. Nine of those who responded (10 percent) charge a fee for classes or workshops. Eight respondents charge a fee for equipment use, while six charge a membership fee. Five respondents indicated that they necessitate that patrons bring their own supplies to the makerspace, and one noted that they only charge patrons for broken equipment.

Putting It All Together

Budgeting for and funding a makerspace is not necessarily a quick and easy process. By carefully considering the needed elements for the space, you can create a clear budget to begin an initial operation. Combining several funding sources can then make what looks good on paper truly come to life. Above all, be prepared at all times with the story of why you would like to add a makerspace. Tell it often, and as your makerspace grows into reality, add successful instances to the tale. This will help you continue to find the funding you need.

ⓖ Library Makerspace Profile: Library Maker Services at Penfield Library, State University of New York at Oswego, NY

http://libraryguides.oswego.edu/makers

Sharona Ginsberg, Learning Technologies Librarian, Penfield Library, State University of New York at Oswego, NY

How Did Your Makerspace Come to Be?

Penfield Library's Maker Services began forming gradually, as the library began to support multimedia creation with circulating technology such as digital cameras, tripods, microphones, and so on, as well as sound-proofed multimedia creation rooms for recording and editing. In 2013, the library obtained its first 3D printer through a grant.

In 2015, when Sharona Ginsberg came on board as the new learning technologies librarian, she held focus groups to test the idea of a makerspace and to find out what people on campus might be interested in. She then successfully applied for a grant from the school to purchase an array of maker equipment for the library, including items such as littleBits, Arduinos, knitting and crochet supplies, a Silhouette Cameo, and more. This was supplemented with donated items such as a sewing machine and stop-motion animation kit. The library began to hold maker events in 2016, followed soon after by the founding of a student Maker Club. Currently, the library puts on maker events, the

Maker Club meets regularly for students, and some of the maker equipment is available outside of these scheduled times by appointment. The library has also begun to circulate some of the maker equipment.

Who Uses It?

The maker equipment is open to everyone: faculty, staff, students, and the local public. Students are the most frequent users and attendees of the maker events. Most of the students at SUNY (State University of New York) Oswego are at the undergraduate level, so undergrads form the majority of the participants, followed next by campus staff. So far, there has been low attendance from faculty. Sometimes, attendees who are affiliated with the campus will bring children, friends, or relatives to the events, which is encouraged.

How Do You Market the Makerspace?

The library's Maker Services has a website (LibGuide) where events are advertised and details regarding services and equipment are provided; this site is linked to from the library website. For each event, Ginsberg creates and posts flyers on campus, including on digital signage. There is an e-mail list for the Maker Club, as well as an e-mail list that staff, faculty, and the public can sign up for to be notified of upcoming events. Events are also advertised in the campus's daily mailing list digest. The most effective promotion so far has been through word of mouth.

Who Supports It?

The learning technologies librarian is primarily in charge of the maker equipment, events, and services. Ginsberg is assisted by the Maker Services Committee made up of three librarians and one staff member, as well as by her student worker assistant. Ginsberg is currently looking for ways to scale the program and offer more support through student workers or interns.

What Does It Include?

The program is mainly event based. The main maker events are hosted by the library. The program also offers workshop tracks—in other words, workshops that include a number of sessions that cumulatively work toward a project. These workshop tracks are sometimes led by librarians but often are collaborations between the library and another unit or an individual on campus with a special hobby or interest. Some examples: a workshop track that teaches attendees to crochet a scarf over four sessions, or one that teaches attendees to set up and start using a Raspberry Pi over three sessions.

Maker Club is an official student organization and meets every other week in the evenings. Club members can gather to use the maker equipment and work on projects together. Maker Club has also collaborated with other student groups on campus; in one recent partnership, they helped the campus Black Student Union create decorations and props for an event.

Outside of events and the club, the equipment is available by appointment based on Ginsberg's availability. Some of the maker equipment is in circulation and can be taken outside of the library.

How Do You Stay Aware of Developments in Makerspaces

Ginsberg mainly keeps up on the field through listservs, blogs, publications, and social media groups. She also runs MakerBridge, an online community and blog for makers that focuses on libraries and schools. Writing regularly for MakerBridge helps her keep on top of what is happening lately in makerspaces.

Many of the decisions about Penfield's Maker Services also get made based on the input of the campus community. Ginsberg does her best to stay aware of other STEAM projects, programs, and events on campus, and to meet with anyone on campus with a personal or professional maker interest. She also attends local Maker Faires and has joined the burgeoning New York State makers community.

What Do You See Happening in Your Makerspace in the Next Year?

Ginsberg is hoping for even more collaborations and partnerships on campus, and hopes to plan more workshop tracks with these partners. Maker Club, still relatively new, will hopefully expand and begin taking on even more interesting projects. Ginsberg will also be putting concentrated effort into bringing the Maker Services to faculty, both for their own benefit and to encourage them to assign their students projects that can take advantage of the library's maker equipment.

Ginsberg has also been working on a partnership with the local public library, and there are plans in the works to hold workshops there aimed at the general public.

What Is Your Advice to Others Who Would Like to Create a Makerspace?

Start small and move along step by step. It's not necessary to get a huge amount of equipment to start with, or even to have a dedicated space. Work with what you have.

Talk to your community and make sure you listen. There is no such thing as a one-size-fits-all makerspace, and there is no such thing as a standard list of equipment to purchase. Not every makerspace needs a 3D printer or any other specific tool. Let the makerspace be formed by the interests of the local community and the people who will be using the space. Even once the makerspace has been created, continue to ask questions and to listen. Form partnerships and collaborations. The makerspace should be a community-driven effort.

⦿ Library Makerspace Profile: Makerspace at Town 'N Country Regional Public Library, Tampa-Hillsborough County Public Library System, Tampa, FL

http://www.hcplc.org

Heidi Colom, Youth Services Librarian, Town 'N Country Regional Public Library

How Did Your Makerspace Come to Be?

The library's supervisor and the regional chief recognized the need for a makerspace. So the supervisor and one of the youth services librarians (Heidi Colom) set up a basic

Figure 5.4. Town 'N Country Library Makerspace. *Photo courtesy of Heidi Colom.*

maker area with a table and chairs plus coloring pages and crayons. The moment it was set up, children immediately flocked to it. More supplies were added gradually and that space remains extremely popular.

Who Uses It?

The Makerspace is in the children's library. It is used by children of all ages. Crafts and building blocks are suitable for ages three and up.

How Do You Market the Makerspace?

Colom and her colleagues mainly market through word of mouth. The Makerspace is in an easily visible location. The moment it was installed, it became very popular. Colom also posts pictures of the Makerspace on social media pages in order to document the additions and updates.

Who Supports It?

The building blocks and the magnetic message board were purchased by the Friends of the Town 'N Country Regional Library. Other supplies come from the library's craft supply budget. The library already had the table and chairs. While Colom is the one in charge of maintaining it, all other staff members help with the restocking of coloring sheets and other art supplies—and everyone can suggest ideas.

What Does It Include?

The Makerspace includes coloring pages, colored pencils, and crayons on a regular basis. Once or twice a month, a craft with supplies is added—usually after a Wee Artists or Creative Artists program. It also includes two types of building blocks: Goldieblox and Magformers. Finally, it has a magnetic message board with magnets in order for children to display their artworks and for the librarian to write seasonal messages.

How Do You Stay Aware of Developments in Makerspaces?

Colom uses social media, professional journals, websites, and books. She has also visited other libraries in order to check out their makerspaces, one of which was the Palm Harbor Library, which has an amazing makerspace with many supplies and activities.

What Do You See Happening in Your Makerspace in the Next Year?

Colom hopes the library can obtain a third type of building block, as well as more art supplies and crafts so that both the analytical and creative aspects of learning can be engaged.

What Is Your Advice to Others Who Would Like to Create a Makerspace?

Rome was not built in one day—and neither is a makerspace. You can start with the very basics, and it will still be in high demand. Keep adding more supplies and activities gradually. Finally, do not forget the left side of the brain: building blocks are very suitable for the analytical minded. Always make sure to replenish the supplies; they will be used up faster than you would think.

Key Points

Makerspaces are about tools, creativity, and community, but they also require money to get started and continue. Here are some key points from the chapter:

- Budgeting for a library makerspace is a key part of the planning process.
- Makerspaces can come together with a combination of internal and external funding along with donations of equipment and materials.
- Library makerspaces face the choice of charging or not charging fees and the subsequent question of which activities will have a charge.

Now the process of creating the makerspace will yield to five chapters that discuss particular types of making, starting with resources for audio, image, and video creation.

References

Bronkar, Cherie. 2017. "How to Start a Library Makerspace." In *The Makerspace Librarian's Sourcebook*, edited by Ellyssa Kroski, 3–28. Chicago: American Library Association.

Ginsberg, Sharona. 2017. "Sustainability: Keeping the Library Makerspace Alive." In *The Makerspace Librarian's Sourcebook*, edited by Ellyssa Kroski, 325–344. Chicago: American Library Association.

Maker Media. 2013. *Makerspace Playbook, School Edition.* http://makerspace.com/wp-content/uploads/2013/02/MakerspacePlaybook-Feb2013.pdf.

Makerspaces.com. 2016. "Makerspace Materials." https://www.makerspaces.com/wp-content/uploads/2016/11/Makerspace-Materials-Supply-List.pdf.

Milwaukee Makerspace Wiki. 2017a. "Equipment List." http://wiki.milwaukeemakerspace.org/equipment.

———. 2017b. "Training Checklists." https://wiki.milwaukeemakerspace.org/miscellaneous/training-checklists.

CHAPTER 6

Resources for Audio, Image, and Video Creation

UNTIL THIS POINT WE HAVE FOCUSED ON the modern maker movement and how that can be merged with libraries. Next, we will turn our attention to discussing distinct maker technologies and activities and look at ways that libraries can incorporate both into their own spaces and programming. This chapter will focus on media creation using audio, video, and images. Exciting activities such as green screen video techniques, stop-motion animation, podcasts, and digital photography are all excellent opportunities for libraries to encourage making of this type. In the informal survey of library makerspaces conducted for this book, this category of making accounted for 369 of the 2,168 activities chosen by the 219 respondents (17 percent). There are countless possible projects for your library to undertake with these types of making.

Making Possibilities

To begin, brainstorm the various projects that a patron could complete; this will provide an end goal for you. If a patron in your library wanted to take on one of these types of audio, image, or video making, what would he or she need? By no means can this list of projects be all-inclusive given the ever-imaginative minds of people. The hope is to suggest some possibilities for making in this area that are feasible and have succeeded elsewhere. See what intrigues you from the list that follows.

Digital Photography and Editing

Maybe your patrons want to try their hands at taking pictures and then learn how to adjust the resulting images into something more aesthetically pleasing or even more creative. Perhaps they want to learn to crop images and adjust the contrast or brightness of images. The library can provide support and instruction on using digital cameras, adjusting settings, using additional light sources, gaining a photographer's eye to frame the perfect shot, and editing images to get the best final image. There are many directions to take this work, and the nice thing for both the library and the patron is that there are multiple levels of complexity to pursue. People can start with the basics and progress through classes or advice from the makerspace staff. The makerspace can then be built up with more advanced tools as the makers come to need them.

Sample projects with image creation could include having patrons take pictures against a green screen and then showing them how to electronically substitute various backgrounds in the image (see figure 6.1). You could have patrons bring in an image as an electronic file or a printed image to scan and then have them use image-editing software to clarify or modify the image in some way. The library could also provide important educational guidance to patrons by teaching them about copyright and images, as the

Figure 6.1. What you see versus what we see. *Image provided through a CC BY 2.0 License by Category5 TV, http://www.flickr.com/photos/category5tv/6508366751.*

Penfield Library at SUNY Oswego did through presentations on using Creative Commons images. Another useful skill for patrons to learn is how to resize and post images to social media sites or for use on their own websites. There could be assignments or practice class projects in school or academic libraries where students take images related to what they are studying and share them with the class through presentation software or in the institution's learning management system.

Audio Recording and Editing

Audio recording gives patrons the ability to create a record of their words and voices, to share their thoughts with others, and perhaps to have a big break with their musical talents. Participants in an audio recording–equipped makerspace can learn about the various options that they have for recording audio and how to increase the quality of the recordings they are making. A lot of ground can be covered, from working with various types of microphones, to choosing how to share and archive audio files, to getting patrons to use their voices effectively to convey information and emotions. On the editing side, makers can learn how to edit out pauses and "umms," change the order of recorded segments, and mix audio files together. See figure 6.2 for an example of what this might look like.

Potential audio projects include patrons recording their thoughts for the purpose of sharing them with others as a podcast. Patrons could also interview family members or record their own memories to share as oral history. They could even combine audio recording with still images and create screencasts, which are useful for providing step-by-step instructions and demonstrations of activities, as well as an easy way to narrate a set of pictures or presentation slides. Patrons in a wide range of ages might be interested in having a location to record music. Of course, the noise-canceling qualities of your space can influence the types of activities that you support. Before you decide to create a sound

Figure 6.2. Group audio recording room. *Image provided through a CC BY 2.0 License by Teaching and Learning with Technology (psutlt), http://www.flickr.com/photos/psutlt/6803213187.*

studio, you need to think carefully about whether you want to have someone play the drums in your library and how you will reduce the sound.

Video Recording and Editing

Video-related making can happen through equipment that the library allows patrons to check out, but it can also happen in a makerspace within the library building. There are many techniques that patrons can discover with fun and practical uses. As with other kinds of making, a skill can be introduced with a recreational project but then called on for other purposes. A green screen can be set up in the library to provide alternative backgrounds to filmed scenes or to create the effects of flying or driving behind those persons being filmed. Stop-motion animation of real-world objects can be recorded with a table and a backdrop. Animated images can also be created in software and used in a video. Once your users have captured video content, you can provide them the means to edit their video on standard public computers in the library or on specialized computers with greater speed and capacity for manipulating large video files. Recorded video can be cropped and reorganized and have effects added to it, along with music and audio files. See figure 6.3 for an example of a video-recording space.

Possible projects involving video include capturing all manner of activities with a camera and then using editing techniques to shape what has been captured. There are many different directions to go, given the number of mobile devices and cameras that can capture video and the options for editing with software on desktops, laptops, and mobile devices. Patrons can make stop-motion videos by assembling scenes out of paper or drawing them on a white board—like the example from Make It @ Your Library at http://

Figure 6.3. VentureBeat video studio. *Image provided through a CC BY 2.0 License by Dylan Tweney (dtweney), http://www.flickr.com/photos/dylan20/6120889483.*

makeitatyourlibrary.org/technology/make-your-own-stop-motion-movie#.Uum2ed-K1GSo. They can create their own music videos, adding effects after filming through the use of a green screen or video-editing software. Students can be filmed reading poetry, creating memorable ways to review coursework, creating public service announcements based on course research, and practicing conversations in a new language they are learning. Patrons could be shown how to film and edit video and then how to post it on YouTube or Facebook to share it with a wider audience. Video projects give patrons a way to communicate their ideas and their creativity while learning technology skills.

One video-related project to add on here is the conversion of older video formats into newer ones. Patrons may have home movies on VHS videocassettes that they need to move to a more modern format so that the movies can still be viewed. With the demise of VCRs behind us and perhaps the end of DVDs not so far off, the next-best format may just be converting to a video file on a flash drive. There are certainly copyright and licensing considerations to consider here (i.e., you cannot make a DVD copy of a VHS version of a title that others hold the copyright on), but it is a service that can aid your community.

⊚ Supplying for Audio, Image, and Video Creation

Since there are so many options for equipment and software, it is best to start at ground level and build upward to higher-quality results with more advanced products. While many types of media creation can now be achieved through smartphones or tablet devices, other items such as high-quality cameras and audio equipment, professional image editing software, and green screen equipment will likely be outside the budgets of your community. Another element to consider is that many of the tools that you might gather for these activities have other uses in more traditional library operations. They may already be on hand in the library—from computers and basic image and sound editors to iPads, microphones, and other items. You could also buy microphones and webcams for the makerspace, for instance, and then have your patrons or staff use them for Skype or Google Hangouts or other web-conferencing options. While some tools might be specialized, the majority will have multiple functions or purposes.

⊚ Image, Audio, and Video Creation Tool Categories

- Computers or mobile devices
- Cameras
- Audio-recording/editing software
- Image-editing software
- Video-recording/editing software
- Accessories

There are some key categories of equipment that library staff will need in order to offer image, audio, and video creation in their makerspace. Those categories are listed in the textbox and then examined at greater length here. Finally, technology needs in this area will be illustrated using the metaphor of the sliding scale to describe basic, enhanced, and advanced combinations of tools that can be offered.

Computers or Mobile Devices

Computers, tablets, or other mobile devices such as smartphones can be used for multiple facets of the image capture and editing process. Desktop and laptop computers (Windows, Macs, Linux, and Chromebooks) can handle the software that is needed to record and edit, and they can be used to plug in additional microphones, webcams, and other devices for recording purposes or to download saved images or video. Tablets (iPads, Android, and Surface) and smartphones generally have microphones and cameras built in and, being mobile, can go wherever the need to record takes you. They can also have apps installed on them to edit audio and video files.

A major consideration for media production with computers and similar devices is processing power and memory. Image, audio, and video files are generally rather large and require enough space to store them in a computer's hard drive or flash memory. This memory need can be alleviated to some degree by using cloud-based storage that puts the files on remote servers rather than keeping them on the local device. But another type of memory demand comes into play when you want to edit or otherwise modify the files. Sufficient RAM (random-access memory) needs to be available in the device to run editing software and process changes to the files.

Cameras

Many types of cameras can be used. Already mentioned are smartphones, tablets, or other devices (e.g., drones) that have built-in cameras and can easily share the images or video they record. Inexpensive point-and-shoot cameras can be used for still images or video recordings, which are then downloaded to a computer for editing or sharing. Additional lenses and peripherals such as flashes can be added to digital SLR (single-lens reflex) cameras to get higher-quality still images and video. Digital camcorders at various price points offer the potential for higher-quality video than what mobile devices can produce. GoPro cameras are small but rugged HD cameras that are often housed in waterproof cases and can be worn or mounted on helmets, handlebars, tripods, and so on to record various activities. Traditionalists may opt for the ever-rarer experience of film cameras, especially if part of the makerspace draw is a darkroom.

Factors to consider when choosing cameras are very much tied to the type of projects that you expect to take on. Camera resolutions are improving across the board, with iPads and iPhones giving higher-definition images than cheaper point-and-shoot cameras or smartphones. If you are after ease of use and are not too concerned with high-quality images—say, if you are posting fairly small-dimension images online—then mobile devices will be sufficient for many purposes. If you want to engage in higher-quality images or video outputs, such as photography for printed objects or the ability to capture video in lower-lighting situations, then you will need to go more in the direction of digital SLR cameras and higher-end camcorders. The ability to zoom and the amount of zoom that you have available with the camera are distinguishing factors, as is the speed of response from the camera, which can give you a clearer picture and a more stable image. Memory, which will generally be flash memory located within the camera, is another feature to watch for in an attempt to obtain the most you can with a device.

Audio-Recording/Editing Software

Software for recording sound will again vary depending on the purpose for the recording. Computers and tablets generally have built-in apps or software to capture audio recordings, or they have free or inexpensive options available for download. For example, Audacity is a free piece of software that runs on many devices and allows you to edit audio files. GarageBand is free software for MacOS and iOS devices that enables multitrack music recording and editing. In the middle, there are many inexpensive apps and software to download, such as Sony Sound Forge (Windows, Mac) or a nonprofit license for Reaper. For something a good bit pricier, Adobe Creative Suite includes a variety of software items to meet your media creation needs, including Adobe Audition for sound recording. Beyond the products mentioned here, if you are pursuing more serious music recording, you might want to explore more expensive recording and mixing software and equipment.

Image-Editing Software

A wide range of software is available to transform digital images. Very basic image editors come with all computer operating systems. There are freeware tools such as GIMP (GNU Image Manipulation Program) for Windows and Mac and Picasa for Windows, Mac, and Linux that can expand your capabilities in this area. Pixlr is a free app for Android and iOS devices; it is also a web-based image editor that can add effects and modify images. Pixelmator is a low-cost tool for Macs, and Corel PaintShop Pro is in a similar price range for Windows. Once again, on the more expensive side, you could consider Adobe Photoshop, which is part of Adobe Creative Suite, for more involved editing and overlaying of effects.

Video-Recording/Editing Software

MovieMaker (Windows) and iMovie (Mac) are included with their respective operating systems, or are available for download and will do the trick of editing video and combining audio with video. There are free web-based tools, such as WeVideo (which has an Android app), Animoto, and Lightworks (which can be downloaded for Windows and Linux). On the pricier end, you could buy Final Cut Pro for Mac or Adobe Premiere for Windows and Mac. As with all the various editors suggested in this section, it is best to try out some of the free resources and see if they can handle your needs, before you sink a significant sum of money into software that might see only occasional use.

Accessories

This catchall category includes a range of items that can assist in media production. Microphones are often built into the devices mentioned previously, but there may be a need to add separate microphones, cabled or wireless, to meet your audio- and video-recording needs. Stand-alone digital audio recorders provide a mobile means for capturing audio, although this function is widely available in mobile devices. The more equipment that you add to a recording space, the more need you will have for stands to hold microphones and for tripods to hold cameras and other recording devices. Green screens are mentioned throughout this chapter, and they come in a variety of price points, from painted sheets that you can make yourself to portable screens that come with a stand. Lights are also useful to enhance the results of video production and photography. One other device that you might want to add to a computer is a scanner to convert printed images or other print matter into digital items.

Sliding Scale for Implementation

Here are three lists of items to add to a makerspace that can take on different levels of complexity in projects. On the basic end, you could get started with the following items:

Computer: Windows Desktop or iMac with 8–16 GB of RAM

Cameras: point-and-shoot digital cameras, inexpensive camcorders, smartphones

Audio-recording/editing software: Audacity or other free editors

Image-editing software: GIMP or other free editors

Video-recording/editing software: MovieMaker or iMovie or other free editors

Accessories: digital audio recorders, scanner

Taking it up a notch, you could add to (or replace) items from the previous list with these products:

Computer: add additional RAM, increased hard drive or flash drive storage

Cameras: iPads, Android tablets, or smartphones; higher-end camcorders

Audio-recording/editing software: Sony SoundForge

Image-editing software: Corel PaintShop Pro or Pixelmator

Video-recording/editing software: Final Cut Pro or Adobe Premiere Elements

Accessories: microphones and stands, lighting kits for video production

Finally, you could work in some of the following items to add to your options and capabilities:

Computer: a dedicated Mac workstation (or multiple ones) for various media production needs, dedicated server space to archive and share digital files

Cameras: digital SLR cameras

Audio-recording/editing software: Adobe Audition, Reaper, or Sound Forge Pro

Image-editing software: Adobe Photoshop

Video-recording/editing software: Adobe Premier

Accessories: a wide array of microphones for various needs, a large-bed scanner for scanning larger items

◎ Maintaining the Makerspace

Fortunately, much of the capture, editing, production, and sharing of final products uses device memory, hard drives, and cloud-based servers, so there is not much to replace on a regular basis. There are fewer memory-holding media items (e.g., cassette tapes, CDs) to use that might get damaged or wear out from repeated use, except perhaps SD (secure digital) memory cards for some devices. The devices themselves will die out eventually, but so long as your patrons are relatively careful with them, you will not need replacements for a few years. You might need to replace microphones every now and then; likewise, you will need a supply of headphones or earbuds for people to use (or purchase) to listen to their creations in the larger library space.

◎ Allocating Space

A positive of this type of making is that the space is very flexible; for instance, using a single tablet to capture sound and video and then edit that content and share it does not take much space at all. If you are going to work with props or animate objects, you will need a little room to spread things out while recording them. The same goes for working with a green screen or other backdrops for photography or video. Adding sound to the equation definitely pushes the dial toward "we need a room for this." In terms of not disturbing others in the library and, even if you have a separate room for a makerspace, not disturbing other makers or having them disturb you, sound projects tend to require some sort of quiet space to record.

You might already have some sort of flexible space in your library, such as a meeting room or study room that may be reserved for a sound- or video-recording session. Most of the equipment that you need can be quite mobile. If that sort of space is not available, then you should pursue converting some existing spot in the library into suitable space.

◎ Library Makerspace Profile: Imaginarium, Mead Public Library, Sheboygan, WI

http://www.meadpl.org/services/imaginarium-digital-media-lab

Ann Miller, Makerspace Coordinator, Mead Public Library

How Did Your Makerspace Come to Be?

The growing trend of makerspaces in libraries piqued the interest of Mead Public Library staff a few years ago, as this was an opportunity to enhance the library's vision "to enrich, educate, connect, create and inspire." In spring 2014, several staff members involved in programming decided to test the waters through an all-ages program called Make It @ Mead and through a family day of making named Sheboygan Connects, which featured a range of activities including stilt walking, a cooking demonstration, broom making, all-age coloring, orchestra conducting, face painting, and children's crafts.

Make It @ Mead made its debut in October 2014 with open studio time in the loft meeting space, on the third floor of the library, with tables offering an array of drawing, painting, jewelry, scrapbooking, stamping, and knitting supplies. By starting with open studio time, and by surveying program attendees that year, Mead staff members were able to gauge areas of interest and proceeded to use those results to apply for a $5,000 grant from the Kohler Foundation in November 2014.

The grant received from the Kohler Foundation was for $2,500 and was matched by the Mead Public Library Foundation. Additional funding was provided by the Friends of Mead Public Library and the Institute of Museum and Library Services through a Library Services and Technology Act grant. This startup funding was used to purchase our makerspace equipment. An additional $2,000 was granted by the Green Bay Packers Foundation to start a digital media lab for teens.

From there, Make It @ Mead developed into a monthly themed craft program, starting with programs that introduced the new equipment to the public, such as cutting silhouette portraits from scanned or digital photos with the Silhouette Cameo and 3D printer demonstrations. Soon after, teen craft and tech programs joined its ranks utilizing the 3D printer and the Arduino and LilyPad kits. The Mead Knitting Circle also began meeting monthly for knitters and crocheters, and the Mead Public Library chapter of the Book to Art Club, invented by Incubator Project founders Laura Damon-Moore and Erinn Batykefer, began meeting monthly for those interested in creating while discussing the monthly read.

In 2016 a space was cleared on the second floor of the library and dedicated for making activities and to house the new equipment. Ann Miller accepted the position of makerspace coordinator, the space was named the Imaginarium through patron voting, and the Imaginarium received a ribbon cutting ceremony by the Sheboygan County Chamber in October 2016. Tours entitled Meet Your Makerspace were given in summer and fall of 2016, and open studio times, called Tinker Time, became regular events throughout each

Figure 6.4. Necktie cuff bracelets at the Imaginarium. *Photo courtesy of Ann Miller, Mead Public Library.*

month. The Imaginarium equipment was available for use through a checkout process when Tinker Time and classes were not in session.

Additional STEAM programs and clubs developed, and continue to develop, including adult STEM classes, Sunday Crafternoons, Bauble Heads Jewelry Club, Ada Lovelace Day, Letterboxing and Geocaching, and classes led by local experts. The Imaginarium also provided journal and button making workshops for teens during the Sheboygan Children's Book Festival.

Collaborations have developed between the Imaginarium and the John Michael Kohler Arts Center's ARTery, Bookworm Gardens, Lakeshore Technical College, and some of the local schools. Additionally, as part of its community outreach program, local chemical lab MilliporeSigma provides their scientists to lead a monthly hands-on, science lab for all ages called Curiosity Labs.

In summer 2017 the Imaginarium hosted its first after-hours making program for adults, Late @ the Library, with assistance from the Étude Group, MAKER Break, Red Raider Robotics, and Bookworm Gardens, and participated in the MAKER Break teen makerspace internship program. The Imaginarium will also initiate its badging program for some of its equipment, such as the 3D printer, sewing machines, and Silhouette Cameo, to ensure proper and safe use of those machines.

Who Uses It?

The Imaginarium hosts all ages in various making and fixing activities. Families, teens, college students, senior citizens, school groups, and a quilting club have all been regular attendees. It often has people walking around to check things out and then staying to color or make the monthly themed project, such as yarn bombing, paper flowers, or blackout poetry. At any given time, patrons may be seen hemming pants, 3D printing, Silhouette cutting scrapbook shapes, or using the iMac lab and Adobe Creative Suite.

How Do You Market the Makerspace?

The Imaginarium and its activities are promoted through social media, the library website, local newspapers, posters, the library newsletter, and word of mouth. Reaching out to the community to teach classes in the Imaginarium or to host library activities has provided additional free advertising.

Who Supports It?

As of this writing, the Imaginarium was still in its first year and was sustained by a portion of the library's programming and book purchasing budgets, funding from the Friends of Mead Public Library, and donations of money and supplies from community members and local businesses, such as Wigwam, which donated socks for the Imaginarium's sock monster and sock monkey classes, and Luz de Luna, which saved wine corks for the wine cork birdhouse class.

What Does It Include?

The Imaginarium has a gallery space made of book shelves for displaying projects; an Ultimaker 2 3D printer; a Silhouette Cameo precision cutting machine; a laptop; four

Figure 6.5. Wine cork birdhouses at the Imaginarium. *Photo courtesy of Ann Miller, Mead Public Library.*

iMacs with Adobe Creative Suite software; four Apple iPad Air 2 tablets; a GoPro camera; a Canon PowerShot digital camera; a Canon CanoScan scanner with film guides; a desktop PC and DVD/VHS player for digital conversion; a Wacom Cintiq drawing tablet; Arduino and LilyPad starter kits; Raspberry Pi kits; LEGO Mindstorms kits; a sewing machine and sewing supplies; a community loom; a T-shirt press; a button maker; a coloring station; a drill; screwdrivers; wrenches; hammers; Ozobot Bits; Sphero; an assortment of drawing, painting, beading, collaging, jewelry making, and knitting supplies; and basic necessities such as scissors, glue, and paper. The digital media lab includes an iMac with GarageBand software, a MIDI keyboard, an audio mixer, two microphones with stands, and four monitors. The Imaginarium also has a small reference library of making books, many of which tie in with makerspace equipment and classes being offered.

How Do You Stay Aware of Developments in Makerspaces?

Miller and her colleagues stay apprised of new makerspace ideas through online resources, social media, books, seminars, workshops, and word of mouth. The public is always sharing ideas that they are interested in.

What Do You See Happening in Your Makerspace in the Next Year?

In the next year, Miller would like to see a circulating collection of Imaginarium resource books, a coding club, a LEGOs club for adults and teens, ceiling outlets, a sink, a workbench for hardware tools, and a growth in volunteers, outside programmers, and open studio times.

What Is Your Advice to Others Who Would Like to Create a Makerspace?

Tour other makerspaces, comprise a wish list of equipment and programs, and research grants to help cover the expense. Most importantly, listen to your community and its needs. After all, it is the community's library and the community's makerspace.

⊚ Library Makerspace Profile: Studio, UTC Library, University of Tennessee at Chattanooga, TN

http://www.utc.edu/library/services/studio

Bo Baker, Director, Studio, and Emily Thompson, Studio Librarian, University of Tennessee at Chattanooga Library

How Did Your Makerspace Come to Be?

Studio opened as part of new construction in January 2015. UTC Library began plans for a new library in 2007 and over the following three to four years dedicated a ton of time to meeting with various stakeholders around campus, organizing focus groups, deploying surveys, visiting other libraries, and engaging in various other research activities. Among dominant themes were those of collaboration and technology. With the new library poised to be a tech hub for campus, the addition of a multimedia/creative space became a natural extension.

Who Uses It?

Studio is a service point open to any university student, staff, or faculty member for academic work, skills development, or just for fun. Some departments—such as art, communication, engineering, and interior design—were earlier adopters of the space, but Studio currently provides instruction and consultation to a breadth of departments across campus and circulates equipment to nearly all departments and majors.

How Do You Market the Makerspace?

Studio has mostly been successful due to the newness of the building generating higher gate counts and due to word of mouth. The library advertises its workshop series, of which Studio is a participant, and Studio services rotate into ad space on the library home page. Otherwise, Studio has not marketed aggressively.

Who Supports It?

Studio is supported by and reports through the UTC Library. It is staffed by two faculty librarians, two-and-a-half full-time staff, and a cadre of student assistants.

What Does It Include?

Studio features the following:

- Computers: twenty-four high-spec PCs (Windows and Mac) with software to support graphic design, audiovisual production, 3D modeling, and interactive design
- Specialty hardware for digitization

- Production rooms: one for audio and music production and one for photography/videography
- 3D printing services
- Circulating equipment: mostly supporting audiovisual production, but Studio also provides equipment for interactive projects such as microcontrollers and single-board computers
- People: staff that provide help, consultation, and formal instruction for the seventy-six hours per week that Studio is open

How Do You Stay Aware of Developments in Makerspaces?

Studio staff pay attention to developments in the larger disciplines, along with ongoing engagement with patron and class needs. Otherwise, staff consult listservs and colleagues.

What Do You See Happening in Your Makerspace in the Next Year?

In the coming year, Studio will expand its equipment roster to include circulating music production equipment and projectors. In addition, it will dedicate space to room-scale VR. Finally, Studio will take on an additional faculty librarian in order to expand instruction and consultation services.

What Is Your Advice to Others Who Would Like to Create a Makerspace?

Here is a list of tried and true library stuff:

- Start with your best estimate of what collections and services your patrons want and need and work from there.
- Understand your limitations (budget, space, personnel, etc.) and solve the resulting service design problems accordingly.
- Seek out relationships to continue iterating.
- For anything that circulates, think about the user experience for the equipment and package accordingly. If you are unsure about continuous funding, purchase extra accessories up front. Find a balance between making equipment accessible and holding users accountable.

Ⓖ Key Points

Working with images, audio, and video in the makerspace is a great way for patrons to learn skills and show their creativity. Another nice element about teaching these skills, apart from the individual talents that develop, is the ability for participants to then help chronicle what else is made in your makerspace.

- Producing media in a makerspace helps patrons become media creators and not just media consumers.
- Many audio, video, and image creation tools are becoming ubiquitous, but a makerspace can provide access to ones that not everyone has.
- There are media creation tools available at multiple price points, and a library can enter into using them along a sliding scale of options.

Next, the creativity continues with crafts and artistic creations in chapter 7.

Resources for Crafts and Artistic Pursuits

THE PHRASE *ARTS AND CRAFTS* MAY SUMMON images of childhood craft projects such as Thanksgiving handprint turkeys, but thanks to today's makerspace machines such as vinyl cutters, laser cutters, and computer numerical control mills, arts and crafts have come a long way. While this category can and certainly does include handmade crafting, new equipment that can be programmed to cut out, sew, and engrave precise designs automatically using a variety of materials such as wood, fabric, acrylic, vinyl, cardboard, and metal have made this type of making even more attractive to people of all ages.

⊚ Making by Hand

What makes arts and crafts in makerspaces unique is that there are easy entry points and the ability to gain expertise whether you are producing something by hand or using a programmed machine. Makerspaces can feature traditional forms of crafting, such as origami, sewing, or carving; they can also have laser cutters and automated sewing machines. The handmade crafts are ones that can be taken on by amateurs of any age. They are appealing opportunities to offer to anyone who is interested in making something that does not require a huge investment in materials and equipment. This might cut against the idea that library makerspaces can offer (or maybe should only offer) making opportunities that patrons cannot afford on their own. But handmade crafts are not without a requirement for instruction and a need for community support that a makerspace can provide, nor are they necessarily without mess that might keep someone from trying them at home. Combining the ease of entry, the draw toward community, and the satisfaction of completing something with hands and hand tools makes these tasks well fitted to the makerspace ethic.

⊚ Making by Machine

An exciting component of makerspaces is being able to see technology at work in machine-aided crafts. In addition to traditional hand use of sewing machines or woodworking equipment, machines are being used to create items through human programming. Computer numerical control (CNC) devices and laser and vinyl cutters can cut, etch, stitch, and otherwise transform many types of materials following a programmed pattern. They provide the ability to create intricate designs and precise lines and curves that can be difficult for the human eye and hand. The relative ease of creating and adapting patterns and the reduced entry price for this equipment make this an exciting option for making.

⊚ Understanding Arts and Crafts Making in the Survey

The informal library makerspace survey provides a sense of the scope of these activities in library makerspaces. Several of the fifty-five technologies and activities listed in the survey cover the content of this chapter. The broader term *art and crafts* was chosen as an activity in 142 of the 219 libraries (65 percent of all libraries responding). More specific areas of creation included activities related to fabric and sewing (63 libraries, or 29 percent), vinyl cutting (56 libraries, or 26 percent), laser cutting (36 libraries, or 12 percent), CNC machines (20 libraries, or 9 percent), and large format printing (20 libraries, or 9 percent). Other libraries chose woodworking (13 libraries, or 6 percent) and jewelry making (10 libraries, or 5 percent). Eight or nine libraries listed each of the following activities—screen printing, milling machine, and industrial sewing machine—while two to four libraries listed industrial mold making, potter's wheel and kiln, silk screening, and ceramics. All told, the activities collected here under *arts and crafts* totaled 386 of the 2,168 choices of technologies and activities in the survey, or 18 percent.

⊚ Making Possibilities

While there is a wide variety of categories of making that could be covered on arts and crafts in makerspaces, here are some approaches and media that you could work with and the equipment that you might need.

Upcycling

A popular approach to arts and crafts in a makerspace is upcycling, or reusing discarded items. This can connect with an environmentally friendly focus among your patrons; it also reduces the cost of many applications. It might involve changing the purpose of the item, such as filling plastic or glass bottles or containers with dirt and plants to make terrariums. Or it might involve transforming the item by using just part of it or combining multiple discarded items for a new purpose, such as turning old tires into tables and benches; transforming old circuit boards into jewelry; creating lamps out of old skateboards, microscopes, and even action figures; or using shattered pieces of CDs and DVDs to create a stunning mosaic table. A search on Pinterest for the term *upcycling* will yield thousands of additional ideas. There is a wealth of possibilities with upcycling, and it can be a sustainable part of the other types of crafting in this chapter.

Paper

Paper-related creation can take a variety of forms. Given the description of upcycling, the paper involved can include scrap paper or leftovers from a project. Paper-folding methods such as origami can create 3D figures that can run the range from fairly simple shapes to intricate designs (see figure 7.1 for an example). Patrons working on scrapbooks can blend multiple pieces of paper to highlight photos with intricate or distinctive

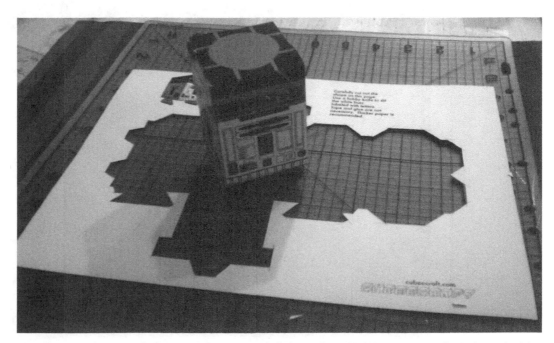

Figure 7.1. Papercraft R2-D2. *Image provided through a CC BY 2.0 License by Kristen Stubbs, http://www.flickr.com/photos/kristenstubbs/3882056033.*

borders. Collages can be created with plain-colored paper or by combining images from discarded periodicals. Posters and signs can be created by etching words or images with a vinyl cutter, by drawing on paper either freehand or with stencils, by printing from word processing or other software, or by screen-printing or silk-screening onto paper with ink and a stencil. You can use paper to prototype various things, such as building methods, by rolling or stacking folded paper to test the durability of a design or aerodynamic concepts (with your old friend, the paper airplane). Papier-mâché transforms old newspapers into creations large and small with the application of paste, supports, and time to dry. Paper is a flexible medium that can also be fairly easy to store.

Sewing/Fabrics

Another popular medium is fabric. Sewing can provide both artistic and practical projects for fabric; it is a skill that can be used to create new clothing, costumes, accessories, and other items and to repair existing ones. Sewing can be done by hand or with a sewing machine that is human directed and operated (see figure 7.2). There are also specialty machines called sergers, which are useful for sewing and cutting the edges of fabric products so that they do not unravel. Taking the machinery a step further, there are CNC sewing machines that can create sewn items from a program. It is interesting to think of the longevity of sewing, given that it features in some of the earliest examples of making in libraries, going back to 1877 ("A History of Making," 2013).

There are many opportunities for upcycling unused or discarded fabric. Screen-printing or silk-screening fabric allows it to take on an image, words, or a complete design. Any making activity involving fabric requires that it be cut, often to precise dimensions to ensure a perfect outcome. Equipment such as laser cutters (which use a laser to burn through fabric) or vinyl cutters (which use a blade) can be programmed to cut exact

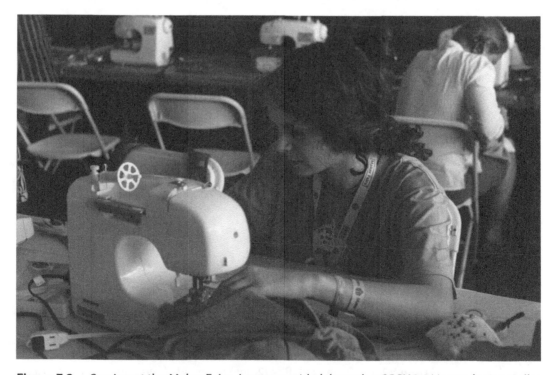

Figure 7.2.   Sewing at the Maker Faire. *Image provided through a CC BY 2.0 License by Jon Callas (joncallas), http://www.flickr.com/photos/joncallas/7230408600.*

patterns to ensure a consistent outcome. Fabric can be stuffed to make pillows, dolls, and a whole host of other possibilities beyond clothing. There are many plans and ideas for fabric at Instructables.com if you search for "fabric," "clothing," or another specific need; there are also ideas on Pinterest.com.

Needlework

It would not be proper to talk of sewing in makerspaces without adding in needlework crafts such as knitting, crocheting, and quilting, which make use of yarn and thread to create items. Groups formed to work on these activities have met in some public libraries for many years. They may work on a large cooperative project, such as a quilt, in which each member contributes a square; they may also gather to encourage one another as they make individual projects. Now, these individuals can be makers who pass their crafts on to other patrons who are new to needlework. There may also be opportunities to combine low-tech needlework with technology, such as sewing LED lights, sensors, and more into fabric to create wearable garments that are interactive. More about wearable technology is covered in the next chapter.

Metal, Wood, and More

Working with more substantial media may not be for every library makerspace. Metal and wood tend to require more equipment and less mobile equipment than the prior media. As covered here, they may well be noisy and messy and require dedicated spaces. But some of these issues vary in severity depending on what you plan to do with metal, wood, vinyl, plastics, and other substances. Hand carving and assembly of wood with glue, hammer, and nail or wire sculpture projects completed with hand tools are not especially messy or loud. But welding a metal frame or using a CNC cutting machine or table saw to cut a piece of wood takes this to another level, in terms of the impact on others in the general area and on heightened needs for safety and training.

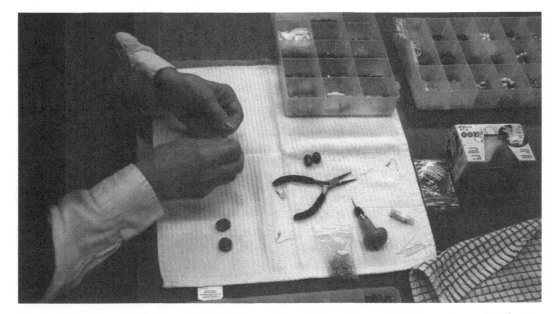

Figure 7.3. Jewelry making at the College of San Mateo Library. *Photo courtesy of Katherine Becvar.*

Notwithstanding these issues, there are some wonderful building and creating opportunities afforded by pursuing these crafts. Wood can be cut by CNC machines to create custom furniture of all types as well as signs, shelves, candleholders, and so much more. Laser cutters are capable of engraving leather and metal as well as cutting wood and acrylic into signs, jewelry, and badges and more. And cardboard can be cut with either type of machine to create tables, lamps, and wall hangings. Rob Dumas details several CNC projects that libraries with makerspaces can offer as activities, such as laser cut name tags, a milled wooden phone stand, and personalized decals (Dumas, 2017). Another possible project is jewelry creating, which can use materials other than wood or metal but can have impressive results when these media are chosen.

Jewelry

Jewelry is another popular product of makerspaces, with many projects available on Instructables.com (do a search for "jewelry" to have a sense of the breadth of options). Jewelry can be constructed from wood, metal, or plastic using laser cutters, woodworking tools, and soldering kits. But jewelry can also be made by hand from beads, shells, ribbons, lengths of cord, and other items. See figure 7.3 for some sample products.

Ceramics

Creating artistic and useful objects from clay is another possibility for the library makerspace. Ceramics involves the shaping of an item from clay and then heating the clay to harden it. Makers can create figurines, tiles, pots, mugs, coasters, key chains, jewelry, and all sorts of other items. Again, a search of Instructables.com for "ceramics" will provide many examples of projects to pursue. Items can be shaped by hand or with handheld tools, or a spinning potter's wheel can be used to shape pots, vases, and other cylindrical items. A kiln is an oven-like device that can properly heat items to harden them. It is a serious investment in ceramics.

⊚ Supplying Craft and Artistic Pursuits Projects

Here are some makerspace items that you will want to have in place to take on the making ideas from this chapter.

CNC Machines

CNC machines can follow programmed patterns to cut, shape, and even sew materials (figure 7.4). They require a connection to a computer to work, along with a design that provides the instructions for how to cut out the lines and shapes. These designs can be created using custom programs such as the Silhouette Studio or Cricut Design Space, which are made specifically for those machines, or alternatively an illustration program such as Inkscape can be used (Dumas, 2017). Long present in large-scale industrial applications, this equipment can now be used more easily by interested individuals due to the availability of smaller and less expensive units, the creation of open sources for patterns, and a growing community of users. In an environment where you want to give patrons the ability to create designs and then produce precisely cut or sewn pieces, CNC machines

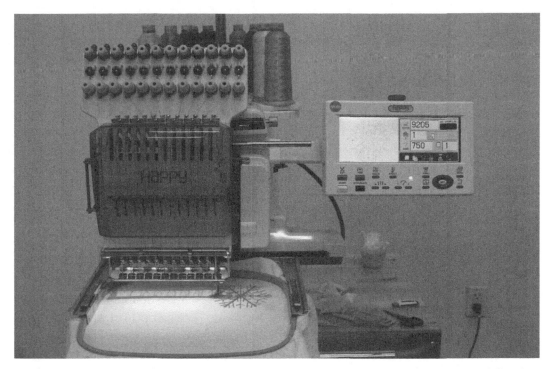

Figure 7.4. CNC Snowflakes 1. *Image provided through a CC BY 2.0 License by Windell Oskay (oskay), http://www.flickr.com/photos/oskay/8305280825.*

provide an exciting opportunity. New desktop CNC machines such as the Shapeoko, Nomad Pro, and Carvey make carving and cutting easy and portable as well as affordable; machines range from $1,000 to $2,500.

Laser Cutters

Precision cutting and engraving are also possible with a laser cutter, which uses a focused laser beam on wood, glass, metal, paper, plastic, and many fabrics at the direction of a CAD (computer-aided design) pattern. Inkscape and Adobe Illustrator are commonly used to create designs, but other CAD programs can be used.

There are different types of lasers to choose from depending on the application that you have in mind, and the latest development in this area is the Glowforge 3D laser printer, which is a laser cutter that can cut and engrave wood, leather, acrylic, fabric, cardboard, paper, and dozens more materials. Since the laser effectively melts the material, harmful fumes can be produced, and some materials may not be suitable for laser cutting, such as vinyl and PVC, as they release hydrochloric acid (Delecki, 2017). The ATX Hackerspace has a great list of materials that should never be used in a laser cutter along with their effects and consequences (ATX Hackerspace, 2017).

Vinyl Cutters

A vinyl cutter has some similarity to the laser cutter but also some key differences. It is computer driven, following a pattern to cut items. It uses a blade rather than a laser, which limits the materials that it can cut. It can handle paper of various kinds and vinyl sheets to produce signs and decals. Software such as Adobe Illustrator and Inkscape or software included with the cutter is needed to input designs and send them to the cutter.

Vinyl cutters come in various sizes, with desktop models available as well. Two of the most popular desktop vinyl cutters are the Silhouette Cameo and the Cricut machines.

Die Cut Machines

With the focus so far on computer-guided cutting devices, hand-operated cutters should not be forgotten. Die cut machines can cut specialized shapes for which dies are created. The die presses into paper that is added to the machine to create multiple copies of the shape. This equipment can be useful in various paper-related making activities, including scrapbooking and sign making. AccuCut and Ellison are leading brands of die cut machines.

Large-Format Printer

Large-format printers are useful for printing large posters and signs. Depending on the printer, they can print to paper sizes that are double the width of standard paper (from 8.5 × 11 inch to 11 × 17 inch), or they can print from rolled paper at a width of 36 inches.

Sewing Machines

Apart from the CNC sewing machines already discussed, human-operated sewing machines are of interest for makerspaces that feature fabrics. Many choices of machines are available, but one consideration is where the sewing machines will be used. If they will be transported to various locations or moved from storage into use on a regular basis, a portable machine is preferable.

Soldering and Welding

Soldering kits can be a useful addition to the makerspace for metal-joining purposes. These kits might be helpful for metal sculpture making or jewelry creation in the arts and crafts area, but they will also be useful in electronics, as discussed in chapter 8. Soldering consists of using a heat source to melt metallic filler that is then placed between two metal items. As the filler hardens, the two items are joined. Welding, however, requires using a heat source that melts the metal on the two pieces that you wish to join, in addition to an added filler. Welding is definitely stepping up a notch in terms of the size of the materials that can be joined and the level of safety that is required to operate the equipment. Welding should be added to the makerspace only if the nature of the work going on there requires that level of equipment. It also requires certification to be able to handle the equipment.

Hand Tools

A variety of hand tools may be useful for the various functions described in this chapter. For most of the arts and crafts activities described here, pliers and scissors are essential items to have for the successful completion of the creation. Note that having multiple pairs of scissors and pliers for instructional sessions is important.

◎ Maintaining the Makerspace

For these activities, refills are a must. Fabric, yarn, paper, glue, metal, wood, clay, and other items will need to be regularly added to the makerspace to keep projects running. Blades will need to be sharpened and regular maintenance performed on equipment. Remember to keep track of supplies and to budget for specific projects. With regular use, the needed supplies will be easier to estimate.

◎ Allocating Space

For these activities, one can expect a wide range of considerations for space, depending on the medium and equipment chosen. Several paper, wood, and vinyl-cutting crafts could be performed anywhere with minimal setup or precautions. But more complex and involved activities and use of larger equipment will necessitate dedicated spaces and additional time and training to succeed in safe making practice. Following are key aspects to consider about space arrangement and preparation with these activities.

Safety

The dangerous nature of cutting and welding equipment requires makerspaces to have the means to separate these items from patrons who are not working on them. Makerspace participants will also need a certification process to prove that they are trained in using such equipment: sometimes a formal certification, at other times the makerspace's own rules to "certify" that someone is ready to use something.

Noise and Dirty Space

Many pieces of equipment are loud and create a lot of waste materials (sawdust, metal shavings, etc.). Even cutting and sewing fabric can leave threads and scraps behind. Those planning the makerspace need to realistically assess how well these issues can be addressed in the space chosen in the library. Occasional noise issues could probably be dealt with for a mobile makerspace holding a workshop here or there; the same is true if dirty space is occasionally required. However, in both cases, if a more regular level of activity is expected (e.g., an open lab), then dedicated space with noise reduction and dirty space capabilities will be needed.

Electricity

For some of the paper or handwork wood crafts, electricity may not be a consideration. But most activities described will require electricity for computers and other pieces of equipment. Hopefully, no one will buy a CNC lathe without thinking out where it will fit in the library and whether there are enough outlets available. Careful examination of the needs and the location will help address this issue.

Room to Spread Out Materials and Equipment

All the activities discussed in this chapter would benefit from having enough space and furniture available to spread out materials and equipment so that materials can be placed, measured, and otherwise prepared for the next steps in the process. This is a common need for activities in the library makerspace.

Ventilation

Many uses of cutting equipment and any operations involving the soldering or welding of materials will require that ventilation be provided to remove toxic fumes from the space (figure 7.5). This will be something to look into as you are considering purchasing equipment and placing it in the library.

Figure 7.5.   Soldering workshop at the College of San Mateo Library. *Photo courtesy of Katherine Becvar.*

🌀 Library Makerspace Profile: The Innovation Lab and Makerspace, Shapiro Library, Southern New Hampshire University, Manchester, NH

http://libguides.snhu.edu/makerspace

Jennifer Harris, Emerging Technology and Systems Librarian, and Chris Cooper, Digital Initiatives Librarian and Archivist, Southern New Hampshire University

How Did Your Makerspace Come to Be?

In October 2013, the Shapiro Library purchased a 3D printer. The decision to pursue 3D printing services was driven by a combination of factors including an institutional desire to increase focus on STEM, an interest in adopting innovative technologies in the library, and incoming support from a newly emerging technologies and systems librarian position.

Figure 7.6. Professor Liz Henley preparing a glass tile for engraving using the Epilog Zing Laser cutter. *Shapiro Library Innovation Lab and Maker-space, Fall 2016.*

At the same time, a new library was under construction, which was conceptualized in 2011. The popularity of the 3D printer led to a decision to change that new library space into one that offered a broader range of technologies and opportunities for creation.

Who Uses It?

The space is open to current Southern New Hampshire University students, faculty, and staff for curricular and noncurricular purposes. Many visitors use the space to experiment with the equipment or build things for personal reasons. However, use of the space to complete class assignments, support non-course-related academic events, or support student clubs and administrative or department events is increasing. For example, between September 2014 and May 2015 approximately 34 percent of 3D print jobs that staff assisted users in printing were to complete a class assignment. Between September 2015 and May 2016, that number rose to approximately 60 percent.

Many student patrons use the space on a one-off basis, for example, to print an object that demonstrates a mathematical theory, print a poster for Undergraduate Research Day, or design and engrave a logo for sport marketing.

Between 2016 and 2017, courses have been developed that use the space and equipment multiple times throughout the semester. For example, a global climate change class used the space to create and improve Arduino-based temperature sensors over the course of a semester. The space has also seen increased interest from faculty who use the space to support their professional and curricular development.

How Do You Market the Makerspace?

The space's audience is internal to the university. Marketing efforts tend to focus on encouraging faculty to use the space for curricular applications. Additionally, the space is marketed to the university community as an opportunity to engage with the technology without specific curricular goals.

Some successful marketing efforts include word of mouth, an e-mail to faculty each semester encouraging use of the space and describing opportunities for curricular applications, and demonstrating successful use of the space through displays, videos, and social media. One-off workshops have largely been phased out as embedded course-specific sessions have reached far more students. The Innovation Lab and Makerspace is highly visible because it is located directly in front of the library entrance. Visibility of the space, the welcoming environment, and expanding to offer many and wide-ranging open hours have also helped encourage use of the space.

Figure 7.7. Student Sophia Beers (class of 2019) displaying a white acrylic mandala she laser cut and engraved for an art and technology class. *Shapiro Library Innovation Lab and Makerspace, Fall 2016.*

Who Supports It?

Library faculty manage the Innovation Lab and Makerspace, including budgeting, planning, purchasing, and marketing. A library staff member and student workers provide the majority of staffing for walk-in hours, equipment and space maintenance, and point-of-need assistance for users. University IT manages the PC, Mac, and laptop computers in the space. Both library faculty and staff hold workshop and class instruction sessions, research potential equipment or software purchases, and ensure rules, policies, and safety guidelines are followed in the space.

What Does It Include?

The space provides access to equipment, software, tools, and consumables. Available equipment includes computers (PCs, Macs, laptops), seven 3D printers, a laser cutter/engraving system, digitization and photography equipment, a sewing machine, a vinyl cutter, board-based electronics (e.g., Arduino, Raspberry Pi), and more. The computers are loaded with 3D printing software, the full Adobe Creative Suite, 3D modeling software (e.g., zBrush, 3DS Max), and other design software. The space also provides access to a wide range of hand tools (e.g., wrenches, a Dremel, soldering irons), crafting materials (e.g., hot glue guns, paints, sewing supplies), and consumables (e.g., super glue, painters tape, LED lights).

How Do You Stay Aware of Developments in Makerspaces?

The library faculty stay aware of developments by following listservs, researching developments and other makerspace offerings, and keeping an eye out for technology trends in library and broader news outlets. Implementation of new technology is informed by university initiatives, curricular developments, and feedback from faculty and students.

What Do You See Happening in Your Makerspace in the Next Year?

The makerspace will expand to support new university programs in engineering, aeronautics, and technology. Equipment and software will also be added to support virtual reality, and library faculty will pursue certification to facilitate drone use for classroom instruction and assignments. Library faculty anticipate a continued increase in student use of the space, a need for more staffing and walk-in hours, and more requests for instruction tied to university curriculum. Library faculty hope to expand the makerspace into an adjacent classroom, creating an environment that combines makerspace technology and instructional space.

What Is Your Advice to Others Who Would Like to Create a Makerspace?

During the planning process for a makerspace, it is important to assess the needs and interests of the audience. In an academic environment, this includes determining the curricular applications of the technologies under consideration and the willingness of faculty to incorporate the makerspace into their courses. There must be strong administrative support, including a commitment to sustained funding for the space, staff, and equipment. Student interest in using the technology for course-related creation and independent experimentation is also key.

Figure 7.8. Professor Liz Henley displaying a mirror she engraved using the Epilog Zing Laser cutter. *Shapiro Library Innovation Lab and Makerspace, Fall 2016.*

It is nearly impossible during the planning phase to anticipate the level of use that your space will generate, and you need to plan for various contingencies, including more or less use than you expected. Have a clear understanding of what you expect users to do in the space and how success can be measured. Consider the realistic capabilities of your audience and the equipment being offered.

⊚ Library Makerspace Profile: Maker Studio, Springdale Public Library, Springdale, AR

https://springdalelibrary.org

Sarah Loch, Young Adult Librarian, Springdale Public Library

How Did Your Makerspace Come to Be?

Springdale Public Library has always offered maker-type programs even before they came to be known by that name. With the growing popularity of and demand for makerspaces, library staff wanted to meet that need for their patrons. They had to think creatively because of their space constraints; every inch of space in their building served at least one purpose, if not more, and their location and the structural considerations of the building make expansion basically impossible.

Library staff rebranded their maker-type programming for teens and adults as Maker Studio. Thanks to funds from the library foundation, staff were able to purchase a wide variety of equipment to support these programs, ranging from sewing machines to a 3D printer, as well as other smaller items that can be used for making and STEAM-based programming.

Who Uses It?

Springdale Public Library makerspace-branded programming is primarily focused on teens and adults, but staff also provide many making-type programs for children, right down to preschool-age patrons. The sewing programs have been the most popular, attracting patrons from teens to senior citizens.

How Do You Market the Makerspace?

The library's primary marketing avenue is through its quarterly newsletter, which lists all the programs. Additional marketing happens through in-library digital and paper signage. News outlets, such as the local NPR affiliate, sometimes pick up items from library press releases and promote them, which is what happened with the sewing programs.

The library has recently hired a marketing director, and staff are hopeful that having a dedicated staff member will open up new marketing avenues and opportunities for these and other programs.

Who Supports It?

All staff members provide direct and indirect staffing support for makerspace programming. Financially, it is primarily supported by the Springdale Public Library Foundation, both through one-time purchases such as the maker equipment and through annual programming budgets that allow staff to purchase materials and pay presenters and instructors.

What Does It Include?

Currently, makerspace programming at Springdale Public Library includes Sew Simple, an adult sewing instruction program that was so successful staff had to add another session to accommodate the interest. For teens, programs range from 3D pens to sewing to a Cosplay 101 series over the summer where teens can create different costume elements, culminating in a costume party at the end of summer programs.

For older children, projects such as sewing are provided, and the library has partnered with a local middle school to offer programs on 3D printing, animation, and other tech-focused making. Makerspace programming for younger children focuses more often on physical making, such as traditional craft projects or building/engineering with LEGOs, to help develop fine and gross motor skills.

How Do You Stay Aware of Developments in Makerspaces?

Library staff stay aware of developments in makerspace programming through following professional publications and online professional communities. Staff also attend professional conferences and cultivate connections with librarians across the country and around the world to share ideas, successes, and challenges.

What Do You See Happening in Your Makerspace in the Next Year?

In the next year, library staff plan to continue with currently offered makerspace programming and also explore new options, especially in self-directed or passive programming. Sarah Loch, the young adult librarian, wants to offer Maker Boxes for teens, allowing

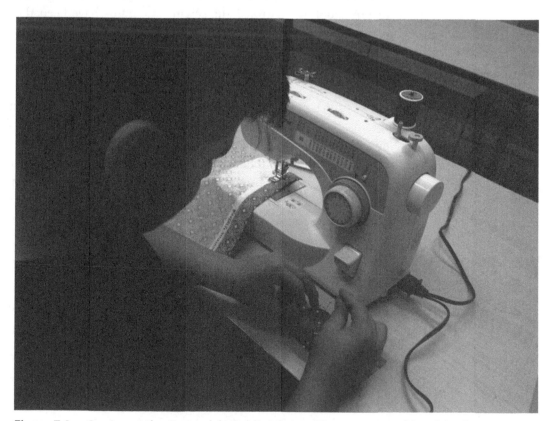

Figure 7.9.   Sewing at the Springdale Public Library. *Photo courtesy of Sarah Loch.*

them to check out equipment and materials, make a small project, and return the equipment for others to use. "One of our primary challenges in teen programming is working around their schedules," Loch said. "Allowing them to check out equipment and create projects on their own time would help overcome that obstacle and give more teens the opportunity to access our makerspace equipment."

What Is Your Advice to Others Who Would Like to Create a Makerspace?

Think outside the box. Just because there isn't a suitable physical place that can be dedicated to being a makerspace doesn't mean you can't provide your patrons with the benefits of maker experiences. Libraries are all about getting creative and working with what they have; if your staff applies that kind of thinking to creating a makerspace, they can make it happen.

Key Points

In considering adding arts and crafts activities to your makerspace, here are some key items to remember:

- Arts and crafts making activities can take a wide variety of forms and levels of complexity.
- Handmade making and machine-assisted making are both very challenging and can turn out equally beautiful creations.
- An exciting element of makerspace arts and crafts is the precision and speed added by technology that brings the capability of making these items to a wider audience of makers.

Now on to forms of making that are less physical and even more dependent on technology, in all of its aspects.

References

ATX Hackerspace. 2017. "Laser Cutter Materials." http://atxhs.org/wiki/Laser_Cutter_Materials.
Delecki, Kevin. 2017. "Safety and Guidelines in the Library Makerspace." In *The Makerspace Librarian's Sourcebook*, edited by Ellyssa Kroski, 73–84. Chicago: American Library Association.
Dumas, Rob. 2017. "Computer Numerical Control in the Library with Cutting and Milling Machines." In *The Makerspace Librarian's Sourcebook*, edited by Ellyssa Kroski, 229–244. Chicago: American Library Association, 2017.
"A History of Making." 2013. *American Libraries* 44 (1/2): 46.

CHAPTER 8

Resources for Electronics, Robotics, and Programming

IN THIS CHAPTER

▷ Understanding Electronics, Robotics, and Programming in the Survey

▷ Making Possibilities

▷ Shopping for Electronics, Robotics, and Programming

▷ Maintaining the Makerspace

▷ Allocating Space

▷ Library Makerspace Profile: Innovation @ the Edge and Innovation Hub, University of Oklahoma, Norman, OK

▷ Library Makerspace Profile: STEAM Central, Stephens Central Library, Tom Green County Library System, San Angelo, TX

ELECTRONICS, ROBOTICS, AND PROGRAMMING go hand-in-hand. Makers can assemble the mechanical components of robots, power them through the use of electronics, and automate them using programming, enabling them to accomplish all manner of tasks. There are many devices and project kits available that serve as an entry point for learning about the basics of electronics and circuitry as well as computers and programming, including visual programming languages. This chapter will explore all three of these and their applicability for library makerspaces.

Understanding Electronics, Robotics, and Programming in the Survey

First, a review of the informal survey results can provide a sense of the scope of these activities in library makerspaces (see the appendix for details). The content of this chapter figured in 27 percent of the choices made from the list of fifty-five technologies and activities in the survey (579 of the 2,168 total choices). At the top of the list was the category of computer programming and software, yielding 106 choices from the 219 respondents (48 percent). In the next most common category, 91 makerspaces (42 percent) featured Arduino and Raspberry Pi microcontrollers. Next came robotics, which is present in 80 libraries (37 percent), followed by electronics, which was chosen by 66 respondents (30 percent). Programming and software to create websites or online portfolios are present in 49 of the makerspaces (22 percent), while soft circuits are in 43 (20 percent). Moving down the list, game creation was chosen by 40 respondents (18 percent), hacking circuits was selected by 35 (16 percent), and electronic book production by 21 respondents (10 percent). The final three were digital scrapbooking, with 20 responses (9 percent); creating apps, with 18 (8 percent); and mobile development, with 10 responses (5 percent).

Ranking the activities and technologies by the percentage of libraries that have them is not meant to connote their value or across-the-board acceptance in library makerspaces. It does show that each has a solid place in multiple libraries. Some of the interactions among them are explored as the types of making are discussed here.

Making Possibilities

To help you explore and implement the broad categories and specific items in the survey results, here is a selection of activities that are practiced in makerspaces involving electronics, robotics, and programming.

Making Stuff to Learn about Electronics

Makers who are new to electronics can utilize kits and sets to learn how things work. More on these in a moment, but there are even more elemental and inexpensive ways to practice working with electronic devices.

A great example of this is building an LED throwie using a small colorful LED light, a 3V lithium battery, a magnet, and some tape. Just tape or epoxy the first three items together, and you have a throwie (named because you can throw it up in the air at night and enjoy the effect). Artists throw them at metal objects, making the objects spur-of-the-moment canvases, and the throwies a form of nondamaging and temporary graffiti (*Wikipedia*, 2017b). This is a pretty simple and cheap experiment (around a dollar) that can build in complexity and create interest. Figure 8.1 gives you an idea of what these throwies look like.

Now back to the kits and sets. There are a variety of products available to help introduce children and people of any age who are new to electronics. Examples of these include littleBits, which offer sets of modules that snap together with magnets. The modules are little circuit boards that serve as connectors, buzzers, switches, pressure sensors, and other elements that can be found in electronic circuitry. By combining the modules with household items such as paper, boxes, tape, LEGOs, and other items, you can create such projects as talking cereal boxes (with flapping tongues) and seascape scenes with mov-

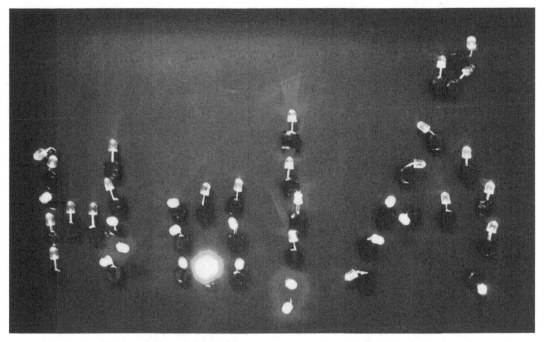

Figure 8.1. LED lights. *Image provided through a CC BY 2.0 License by urban_data, http://www. flickr.com/photos/urban_data/438642086.*

ing construction paper waves, and you can trick out your skateboard with programmed lights (see the examples at http://littlebits.cc/projects or on the Instructables.com site by searching "littleBits"). Along the way, littleBits makers are learning how circuitry works and building up skills to make more complex projects.

A couple of similar products are Snap Circuits and Squishy Circuits. Snap Circuits consist of plastic and metal parts that you lay out on a plastic board. Once they are connected and linked in a circuit, some sort of activity ensues, depending on which components you have added. You can create motion detectors, lights with light switches, various sound-producing items, and even mobile items once you take the circuits from the plastic board and mount them on a vehicle (see more examples at http://www.snapcircuits.net/learning_center/kids_creation or on the Instructables.com site by searching "Snap Circuits"). Squishy Circuits can teach the same skills and produce similar products as these but with the addition of dough. The dough conducts electricity, and the recipe is freely available at http://courseweb.stthomas.edu/apthomas/SquishyCircuits/. The dough can be used to link lights, switches, and other electrical items. Sample projects are available at the website cited or on YouTube.com (just search for "Squishy Circuits").

The main distinctions among the three products are options, cost, and ease of use. LittleBits are more expandable and flexible in terms of the prebuilt modules that they have available and the way that they connect with magnets, but they are more expensive. Snap Circuits are easy to work with, even for younger kids, but have a more limited array of projects. Squishy Circuits can be the least expensive in that the dough recipe is freely available and you are responsible only for providing the electronic components, LEDs, or wires that you add to the dough.

Wendy Harrop provides several suggestions for library circuitry projects to engage patrons, such as creating interactive models, building light-up board games, creating illuminated greeting cards, making creative interactive artwork with paper circuits, and even creating robots using littleBits (Harrop, 2017).

Making Stuff Go

Once the process of connecting electrical components is understood, another activity to pursue is devices that make things happen. The happening can be fairly simple, such as lights that blink, or very involved, such as a robot that can alter its movement in response to the placement of furniture or people who cross its path. These devices, known as microcontrollers, require not only the connection of circuits and devices but also the addition of programming to the equation. Programming allows these devices to operate automatically and independently so that no one has to throw a switch or hold a wire on a battery, as in the earlier electronic examples. What follow are some components that might be used to create projects in this way.

Arduino

Arduinos are little devices that provide a link between hardware (e.g., light sensors, lights, and motors) and the software program that directs the hardware. See figure 8.2 to get an idea of what one is. It is a circuit board that you can plug components into, but it also has the ability to be programmed. It can hold one program, or sketch, at a time. There is a whole library of open-source sketches available that you can use as is or adapt to your specific need and to the components that you are going to use. You can use a USB cable to connect the Arduino to a computer and then use free Arduino Development Environment software to enter your commands and compile and upload the sketch (Smith, 2017). Then you unplug the Arduino, and it is ready to do whatever you told it to do in the sketch. What can you do with it? Well, you can create some incredible light shows with

Figure 8.2.   Raspberry Pi Model B and Arduino Uno. *Image provided through a CC BY 2.0 License by redcctshirt, http://www.flickr.com/photos/redcctshirt/10192600203.*

flashing lights, a rotating globe, and a self-controlled vehicle. There are many interesting possibilities on the Arduino website (http://www.arduino.cc) and at Instructables.com. Jonathan M. Smith offers instructions on several Arduino projects that are appropriate for libraries, such as how to create sketches for a blinking LED light, a traffic light, a temperature sensor, and a room occupancy sensor—including instructions for connecting the necessary components to the board (Smith, 2017). Something that you may find the need for with the Arduino and other electronic projects is a breadboard, which is a piece of plastic with little plug holes in it where you can connect electronic devices without having to solder them together. It is meant as a temporary place to prototype a project. You just plug them in and even plug the Arduino in to direct your project.

Makey Makey

If you are not ready for the whole Arduino experience, you could consider a Makey Makey. This device resulted from a very successful Kickstarter.com campaign in 2012. It is a card that has ports to attach devices, as well as a USB port that you cable back to a computer. Generally, any software that uses the computer keyboard and mouse can be controlled through the Makey Makey—well, not just by the Makey Makey but by whatever you connect to the ports on the device that control the keyboard and mouse. So, you can use alligator clips to connect a banana to the spacebar and touch the banana to use the spacebar. Or you can create a control panel for a game on a piece of paper, with controls drawn with pencil graphite that have alligator clips on them. Aside from existing software, there are programs created for the Makey Makey, and you can create your own with Scratch (an open-source programming tool discussed later). You have to keep the Makey Makey plugged into your computer to access the software and give the device power. Although it is something of a limited version of an Arduino, it can still teach patrons quite a bit about how devices (and even bananas) interact with software.

Raspberry Pi

The Raspberry Pi is similar to the first two devices in this section, but it takes things a step or two further. Not much larger than an Arduino (see figure 8.2), the Raspberry Pi is effectively a credit card–sized computer. You just need to plug in a television, a keyboard, an SD card for added memory, and a network cable to get it on the web. It will work fine as a computer for basic tasks, from making spreadsheets to playing video. You can also use its capacities as a microcontroller by adding programs into its built-in memory. Generally, though, the projects that you might want to undertake with an Arduino are going to be a little more involved with the Raspberry Pi. It has greater capabilities than the Arduino and is a great next step for more complex projects. One source to turn to for projects is the community at Element 14 (http://www.element14.com), and another is to Stephen M. Tafoya's chapter (Tafoya, 2017) on Raspberry Pi for Librarians in which he details how to make music with Sonic Pi, code with Scratch on the Pi, Minecraft hacking with the Kano OS, and how to create a cloud server using Google Coder.

LEGO Mindstorms and Robot Kits

Another route to turn to with making things go is something that is focused on robotics. You can do robotics projects with the Arduino and the Raspberry Pi, but some LEGO

Figure 8.3. LEGO Mindstorms EV3. *Image provided through a CC BY 2.0 License by Franklin Park Library, https://www.flickr.com/photos/franklinparklibrary/22474032354/.*

products are dedicated to that outcome. They tend to be focused more on kids (WeDo for younger kids), but they are a lot of fun. There are many projects for each of their sets on the LEGO site, as well as on YouTube and elsewhere (see figure 8.3 for an example). Makeblock is an alternative that is similar; it sells educational robot kits for different grade levels that can be built and then be programmed using the graphical programming app.

Making E-Textiles

An interesting tilt from the things-that-go and electronics categories are e-textiles, or adding circuitry and automation to fabrics. Two examples to have in mind are soft circuits and projects using the LilyPad, a variant of the Arduino. Soft circuits provide a way to create wearable electronics by adding circuits to clothing and other items. They range in complexity from creating LED cuff bracelets to a light-locked wallet to a plush game controller (Egbert, 2017). The idea is that anything you can do with circuits on a breadboard, you can sew into a garment and have it happen while you wear it. You use conductive thread to connect the components while also connecting the whole product to the fabric. The LilyPad is a microcontroller that is designed for work with textiles, and it offers the ability to locate programming into the process. As figure 8.4 demonstrates, the LilyPad is a lily pad–shaped Arduino that can lie flat in a garment and control the lights and sounds and whatever else you add to the fabric. If you want a pattern to slowly appear on the sleeves of your shirt in neon green and red lights, you can make it happen. There are many exciting projects for both soft circuits and the LilyPad at Instructables.com.

Changing Things with Electronic Devices

A popular activity in makerspaces is to have programs in which patrons take appliances or other devices apart to see how they work and what else can be made with the parts. The next step with this is to add something onto an existing product to make it do more. Toy

Figure 8.4. LilyPad tilt sound demo. *Image provided through a CC BY 2.0 License by Plusea, https://www.flickr.com/photos/plusea/24858206111/.*

hacking is one method for doing this: taking an existing toy and adding circuitry and/or microcontrollers to it to make it look or do something special. From footballs to dolls to radio-controlled cars, the sky is the limit. You can find many examples on Instructables. com. This is an application of the earlier technologies in this chapter to teach people to modify items and upgrade their capabilities.

Programming, Hackathons, and App Development

In addition to being used for tasks in the prior category of making, programming can be an activity taught, learned, and practiced in the makerspace on its own merits. Programming can be used to create games, Internet applications, animations, and more. Scratch and Python are open-source programming languages that are often used in makerspaces. They both have educational uses and are relatively easy languages to learn. This makes them perfect for the makerspace environment. They also both have lots of examples, or libraries, available that can be used or modified as part of a new program. You can learn more about them and find suggested projects by visiting the Scratch (http://scratch.mit. edu/starter_projects/) and Python (http://www.python.org/about/apps/) sites. Libraries can host Hour of Code events that feature introductory coding lessons using visual programming languages such as Scratch and Blockly to introduce kids to programming concepts (*Wikipedia*, 2017a).

Hackathons and other hackerspace programs can be organized in libraries as competitive events or as simple themed activities such as "Minecraft hacking." These types of activities don't even need to involve computer programming and can be as simple as toy hacking, which promotes reverse engineering an object by taking it apart to see how it works and then making it into something new (Clark, 2017).

Another programming direction for makerspaces is to offer instruction and facilities for creating games and mobile apps. Games could be programmed using Scratch or Python for desktops and laptops, and mobile apps can be developed for the Android platform by using the MIT App Inventor 2 platform (Clark, 2017). You can also write apps in HTML and JavaScript. The big questions to start out with are what operating system you will create the app for and how you will distribute it. It is a great project for makers to try creating something that they can download onto their phones and see in action.

Making Websites and Online Portfolios

Another direction to take programming instruction and practice in makerspaces is toward building websites. There are many venues for building an online presence, such as Facebook, Twitter, and blogs, in which you can easily add text and images about yourself and what you are interested in. If you would like to have more flexibility in how you display information online, you can pursue building your own website. The programming language to learn is HTML (hypertext markup language). There are many free website locations out there to host your work, including Google Sites, Wix.com, and Weebly.com. Even if you are going to work within environments where you mostly do not need to program your own HTML, you will find that you can modify existing text by going into the source of a page and tweaking the code. HTML is a lot of fun to work with because everyone makes his or her code freely available for you to sample. There are countless sites that define HTML elements and give examples on how to use them. It is a great skill to teach your makers so that they can control how information about themselves and their projects is shared.

Making E-Books

Another natural area of interest for library makers is creating e-books. It is another form of creation that can utilize various software tools for creating documents, gathering and editing images, and then assembling them into an electronic book. Of particular note in this area is Amazon's Kindle Direct Publishing program, which enables authors to freely and easily self-publish their e-books and reach millions of readers through Amazon. Also worth mentioning is Apple's iBooks Author, which creates e-books that are then available for use on iPads and other iOS devices. Whether for group publishing projects or individual efforts, giving your patrons the potential to self-produce a book can be a very appealing option.

Shopping for Electronics, Robotics, and Programming

What further items are needed (in addition to the products mentioned so far) to turn these activities from ideas to realities? At a minimum, you'll need a computer of some kind (maybe just a Raspberry Pi, a television, and a memory card). Of course, having multiple people working on programming projects and uploading sketches to their Arduinos will require multiple computers. Perhaps you can make use of an existing computer lab in the library for instructing people in these projects. Arduino, LilyPad, Makey Makey, and Raspberry Pi projects will require the purchase of many small electrical components, such as resistors, light sensors, and other devices, as well as wire, conductive thread, and alligator clips. Much will depend on the precise project that you have in mind or how complete an array of options you would like to provide. For the most part, soldering will not be needed for these projects, but that is an option to add on for more involved or permanent circuit board or related constructions. Some basic hand tools (pliers, scissors, and screwdrivers) and sewing items would be helpful.

◎ Maintaining the Makerspace

While many of the materials used in these activities are reusable, there will likely be a need to replace batteries, add tape for throwies, replace wires, and provide textiles and thread. Also, you might want to replace Arduinos or LilyPads as they are put into permanent use in products.

◎ Allocating Space

Your space requirements are all dependent on what making will be done. While the work is not necessarily noisy or dangerous, care must be taken with the electrical elements. Sufficient space is needed to spread out items during assembly of the electronic projects, as is easy access to computers for programming and e-book creation. Working with the electronic items will mean a lot of spare parts and gear to store, and if dedicated space is not available, then there will have to be somewhere to store things. One final thing to consider is the option of circulating Arduino, Makey Makey, and Raspberry Pi kits for patrons to use beyond the library (as is done at many libraries profiled in this book).

◎ Library Makerspace Profile: Innovation @ the Edge and Innovation Hub, University of Oklahoma, Norman, OK

https://libraries.ou.edu/edge

https://github.com/OULibraries/edge/wiki

http://ou.edu/content/innovationhub.html

Carl Grant, Associate Dean, Knowledge Services and Chief Technology Officer, University of Oklahoma

How Did Your Makerspace Come to Be?

For the 125th anniversary, the university held a campus-wide exhibition called "Galileo's World" (OU [University of Oklahoma] Libraries is one of only two locations—the Vatican being the other—in the world holding all twelve of Galileo's first edition works, four of which have Galileo's handwriting in them). One of the exhibits was a VR station allowing people to compare the universe as Galileo thought it existed, with NASA images of how it really exists. It was very popular and became part of an initiative to create a space, in the library, focused on creating new knowledge using new technologies such as VR, 3D printing, microcontrollers, and more. It also helped to support plans for a larger facility on OU's research campus, called the Innovation Hub.

Who Uses It?

The Innovation @ the Edge (250 square feet) is widely used by faculty, staff, students, and the public. As of this writing, a little after a year since the space launched, the university has twenty-five courses with a VR component, requiring students to come to the space to complete the work; Innovation @ the Edge staff has printed over six hundred 3D items, had 292 workshop participants, and had 120 research or pedagogical consultations. The Innovation Hub (20,000 square feet) opened more recently and does not have statistics yet, but given it is considerably larger than the Innovation @ the Edge, staff expect good results.

How Do You Market the Makerspace?

The staff do not call their space a makerspace as they feel that while that is a widely known term, it narrows the focus from what they're hoping to achieve, which is to promote innovation in the creation of knowledge through thought and expression. They market the spaces by focusing on faculty showing an interest in leading-edge developments and on new, incoming faculty looking to achieve tenure. These people tend to be open to new approaches, so the staff work closely with them to show them how the technology of the innovation spaces can advance their research and pedagogy. The staff also introduce the technology in a specific sequence. They start with the library team, then the deans of colleges, next the associate deans, and then staff and students. Faculty are then hearing from people all around them, which tends to lead to them coming to the space to find out what the buzz is all about. The library also partners with the museums on campus, which leads to public tours and use, as well as many local newspaper stories. They have entered products/ideas from these spaces in national contests and have won at least two awards, which helps to generate a lot of good press as well.

Who Supports It?

- Innovation @ the Edge (in the library) is supported by the library.
- Innovation Hub (in the research park) is supported by the OU administration, the vice president of research, the College of Business, the College of Engineering, and OU Libraries.

What Does It Include?

Innovation @ the Edge includes

- Virtual reality (Oculus-Rift, HTC Vive, Google Cardboard units)
- 3D printing
- Robotics
- Microcontrollers
- Software Carpentry
- A mind-set of experimentation and knowledge creation using the preceding items
- Community
- Collaboration

Innovation Hub includes

- Virtual reality
- 3D printing
- CNC (computer numerical control) milling machines

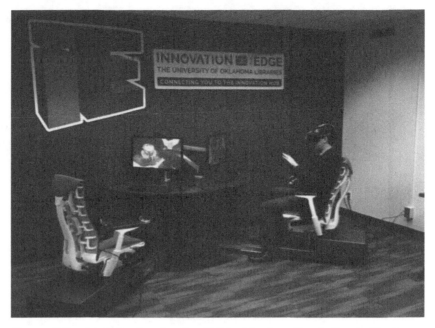

Figure 8.5. Matt Cook using the OVAL virtual reality station in the Innovation @ the Edge. *Photo Courtesy of Carl Grant.*

- A vinyl cutter
- A laser cutter
- Woodshop tools
- Electronics

How Do You Stay Aware of Developments in Makerspaces?

The library staff read periodicals like *MIT Review*, *Wired*, and *Maker:*. They also monitor a wide assortment of blogs and online news sources in the field. Finally, they attend conferences and workshops when and where possible.

What Do You See Happening in Your Makerspace in the Next Year?

The library staff's focus is on building the community of users around the spaces and the staffing for the spaces.

- In terms of staffing, they have a fair number of volunteers and are starting a badging initiative so they can recognize their efforts.
- They are continuing to offer Software Carpentry workshops to bring people into the spaces and learn new coding skills in compact two-day workshops.
- They encourage community members to enter contests like the Knight News Challenge.
- They are launching a larger promotion/press effort that includes social media, videos, conference presentations, professional journals, newspapers, digital signage, and websites.
- They are expanding their robotics efforts and moving toward the support of Internet-of-Things technologies.
- They are working closely with a student-initiated virtual reality association/club.

What Is Your Advice to Others Who Would Like to Create a Makerspace?

- Decide on the goals/objectives for the space and make certain those goals directly link to and support the goals of your library and the community it serves.
- Decide on the metrics that will be measured to ensure success in achieving those goals.
- Decide on the space, hardware, and software that will be needed.
- Think about how you are going to staff the space (full-time employees, volunteers, a combination, etc.)
- Plan the building of the community of users.
- Plan your promotion campaign.
- Ensure you are building a scalable operation, that is, one that can be readily expanded if the community takes to it in the way you are planning.

More Info

Online presentations about the space(s):

1. "What's the Reality of Virtual Reality in a Modern Research University Library?" (https://www.cni.org/topics/assessment/whats-the-reality-of-virtual-reality-in-a-modern-research-university-library).
2. "Scaling Maker Spaces across the Web: Weaving Maker Space Communities Together to Support Distributed, Networked Collaboration in Knowledge Creation" (https://vimeo.com/166081979).
3. "Makerspaces, Virtual Reality, the Internet of Things at Alia Stories," by Karim Boughida, Angelica Ferria, Deborah Mongeau (University of Rhode Island); Brian Mathews (Virginia Polytechnic Institute and State University); Brian Jepson (O'Reilly Media); Carl Grant (University of Oklahoma). Please note: The University of Oklahoma segment is between 23:20 and 38:30. The OU Libraries staff strongly urge anyone interested in creating a space to watch this segment (https://youtu.be/zSJ7KBSsTrA)!
4. A video of projects that have happened in the library innovation space: https://www.youtube.com/watch?v=tmL3T28Ud1k.

Ⓖ Library Makerspace Profile: STEAM Central, Stephens Central Library, Tom Green County Library System, San Angelo, TX

http://www.tgclibrary.com/steamcentralhome.asp

Clint Hudson, Maker-in-Residence, Stephens Central Library, Tom Green County Library System, San Angelo, TX

How Did Your Makerspace Come to Be?

In 2014, Assistant Director Wanda Green began exploring the possibility of creating a community makerspace in four thousand square feet of unused shell space in the Stephens Central Library. When a grant opportunity presented itself, she contacted the city

Figure 8.6. EV3 robotics at STEAM Central, Stephens Central Library, Tom Green County Library System. *Photo courtesy of Clint Hudson @STEAM Central.*

fire marshal's office, the county risk manager, facilities maintenance, and area makers to research the possibilities and limitations of the space and survey the community to discover what types of programs and equipment were desired. With data in hand, Green sought and won approval from the library's governing body to apply for a Texas State Library and Archives Commission (TSLAC) Special Projects Grant for $75,000 to hire a maker-in-residence, purchase equipment and outreach kits, and develop the STEAM Central Makerspace. The grant was awarded, and STEAM Central was born, opening March 23, 2017.

Clint Hudson, the library's new maker-in-residence, and Green maximized grant funds by working within the space limitations, utilizing cast-off furniture from other county departments, accepting community donations of tools, equipment, and consumables, and DIYing as much as possible (they made their own white boards, green screen, tool pegboard stand, and painted the walls). The bulk of the funds were used for equipment: laser cutter with filter system, long arm quilter, embroidery machine, sewing machines, hand tools, soldering stations, spinning wheels, drum carder, small loom, cameras, die cut machines, and various craft and hobby tools and equipment.

Who Uses It?

Any Tom Green County Library System (TGCL) card holder can use the space, and as TGCL will issue a card to any Texas resident, that includes the entire state of Texas! The space has been used by a wide variety of people, from preschool groups using the early childhood robotics resources to the high school robotics teams; from model airplane enthusiasts using the 3D printer and laser cutter to quilters and knitters. Educators bring school groups regularly for special programs and events, and staff work with their area Educational Service Center, Region XV, to educate school personnel.

STEAM Central's partner organizations also heavily use the space—San Angelo Museum of Fine Art, Girl Scouts, San Angelo Chapter of the Texas Alliance for Minorities in Engineering, 4H, Concho Valley Workforce Development Board, Angelo State University's Department of Civil Engineering, Howard College—to name just a few.

How Do You Market the Makerspace?

STEAM Central is marketed directly to members of partner organizations through those organizations. The staff promote STEAM Central to families and educators via brochures sent to public schools twice a year, and directly to the community through local print publications, such as the newspaper and *San Angelo Family* magazine. STEAM Central maintains an active Facebook page, as well as pages on the library's website.

Who Supports It?

STEAM Central was made possible through a TSLAC and Institute of Museum and Library Services grant. Tom Green County, the governing body for the Tom Green County Library, provides funding for maintenance of equipment and a portion of the salary for the maker-in-residence.

Community members have generously donated many consumable materials, such as yarn, beads, and fabric, as well as tools and equipment. Two donations in particular—stained glass tools and consumables and a large eight-harness floor loom—were particularly generous and greatly enhanced the space.

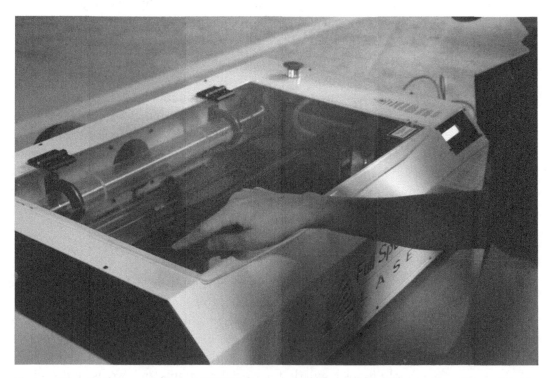

Figure 8.7. Quilting machine at STEAM Central, Stephens Central Library, Tom Green County Library System. *Photo courtesy of Clint Hudson @STEAM Central.*

What Does It Include?

STEAM Central includes several robotics and Arduino kits:

- Eight Dash and Dot Robots with accessories
- Twelve Spheros with accessories
- Six LEGO EV3 Mindstorms
- Eight LEGO We Do 1.0
- Two Hummingbird classroom kits
- littleBits Pro Library
- Ten SparkFun Inventor's Kits

It also includes several manipulatives kits:

- LEGOs, Zoobs, Squibs, Lincoln Logs, and so on
- K'Nex Education (multiple sets with different focuses)
- Snap Circuits
- Keva Classroom 1000
- Strawbees EDU
- MakeDo

There are tools available for use in the space once patrons have been through a safety/training class:

- Textiles: long arm, embroidery, sewing machine, knitting, crochet, felting, spinning, carding, and weaving
- Laser cutter: FSL (Full Spectrum Laser) 5th Gen Hobby Laser, water chiller, BOFA filter
- 3D printer: Ultimaker 2+
- Video/photo: green screen, lighting, and camera (digital single-lens reflex); computers and software for editing photography and videos
- Paper/vinyl/fabric cutting: Cricut Expressions 2 and Silhouette Cameo 3, plus software; AccuQuilt die cutter, Tim Holtz Vagabond die cutter
- Electronics: soldering iron and accessories, multimeter, and so on
- Hand tools: screwdrivers, hammers, pliers, dremels, and so on
- Miscellaneous other tools and equipment: clay, screen printing, jewelry making, and so on
- Software: Adobe Creative Suite, Premier, embroidery software, GIMP (GNU Image Manipulation Program), Inkscape, Darkroom, and so on

How Do You Stay Aware of Developments in Makerspaces?

The staff read periodicals, such as *Make:* magazine; browse websites and blogs; participate in listservs, such as the Texas Innovation Group; follow Nation of Makers; and attend educational programs, webinars, and conferences such as the International Society for Technology in Education and the Texas Library Association Conference.

What Do You See Happening in Your Makerspace in the Next Year?

The amazing aspect of the makerspace is it is community driven. Wanda Green placed poster board in the entrance of the library with the words "I want to make . . . in the library." The response was incredible! Every day more and more people would write things they wanted to create. They ranged from ceramic pottery and stained glass to computer animations. This board has always been the focus of the makerspace and will continue to guide it into the next year. The library's goal for next year is to add audio recording and editing equipment, further develop the outreach kits and capabilities, and develop more partnerships with community organizations.

Figure 8.8. Laser cutter at STEAM Central, Stephens Central Library, Tom Green County Library System. *Photo courtesy of Clint Hudson @STEAM Central.*

What Is Your Advice to Others Who Would Like to Create a Makerspace?

The most important piece of advice would be to survey your community and implement their suggestions. Makerspaces have the potential to change lives and futures, so it is absolutely worth incorporating a makerspace into library services. Community volunteers will always be your most valuable resource. There is such a variety of opportunities for library patrons, and you can't possibly learn everything. That's where community volunteers come to the rescue. They provide the expertise that you absolutely need. The Stephens Central Library has volunteers that teach classes from knitting and drawing exercises to primitive hand-thrown pottery. Always put your patrons and their interests and needs first, and you will have an extremely successful makerspace.

⊚ Key Points

Electronics, robotics, and programming activities can serve a variety of purposes in a library makerspace.

- Patrons can learn the basics of how electrical devices work and how to create simple examples of them.
- Microcontrollers allow for more advanced projects that operate under programmed routines.
- Programming can be taught as a stand-alone activity or used in tandem with other creative activities.

Turn to chapter 9 for a discussion of how items designed in software can be formed into physical objects through 3D printing.

⊚ References

Clark, Chad. 2017. "Library Hackerspace Programs." In *The Makerspace Librarian's Sourcebook*, edited by Ellyssa Kroski, 287–303. Chicago: American Library Association.

Egbert, Megan. 2017. "LilyPad, Adafruit, and More: Wearable Electronics for Libraries." In *The Makerspace Librarian's Sourcebook*, edited by Ellyssa Kroski, 157–173. Chicago: American Library Association.

Harrop, Wendy. 2017. "littleBits, Makey Makey, Chibitronics, and More: Circuitry Projects for Libraries." In *The Makerspace Librarian's Sourcebook*, edited by Ellyssa Kroski, 213–228. Chicago: American Library Association.

Smith, Jonathan M. 2017. "Arduino for Librarians." In *The Makerspace Librarian's Sourcebook*, edited by Ellyssa Kroski, 135–155. Chicago: American Library Association.

Tafoya, Stephen M. 2017. "Raspberry Pi for Librarians." In *The Makerspace Librarian's Sourcebook*, edited by Ellyssa Kroski, 113–133. Chicago: American Library Association.

Wikipedia. 2017a. S.v. "Code.org." https://en.wikipedia.org/wiki/Code.org.

———. 2017b. S.v. "LED Art." https://en.wikipedia.org/wiki/LED_art.

CHAPTER 9

Resources for 3D Printing and Prototyping

IN THIS CHAPTER

▷ Making Possibilities

▷ Understanding 3D Printing

▷ Benefits of 3D Printing

▷ Supplying for 3D Printing

▷ Maintaining the Makerspace

▷ Allocating Space

▷ Considering Intellectual Property

▷ Envisioning the Future of 3D Printing

▷ Library Makerspace Profile: DeLaMare Science and Engineering Library, University of Nevada, Reno, NV

▷ Library Makerspace Profile: ACU Maker Lab, Abilene Christian University Library, Abilene, TX

THE IDEA BEHIND 3D PRINTING is all but magical to most people, much like the notion of conjuring objects out of thin air or transforming base metals into gold. 3D printers are at once mystical and futuristic, invoking images of science fiction television and movies. Watching these machines set down layers of plastic filament to produce a 3D object, one cannot be anything less than astonished. When most people think of makerspaces, they likely think of 3D printers. They are prevalent in the majority of library makerspaces and will continue to be so, given their popularity and increasing affordability. This chapter will discuss the ins and outs of these unique devices. See figure 9.1 for an example.

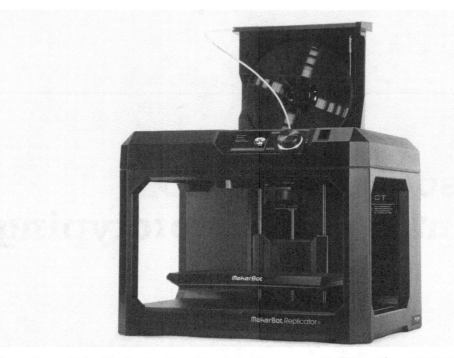

Figure 9.1. MakerBot Replicator+ 3D printer. *Image provided through a CC BY 2.0 License by Creative Tools, https://www.flickr.com/photos/creative_tools/29577315510/.*

The informal survey of library makerspaces (see the appendix for details) revealed that 144 of the 219 respondents (66 percent) offer 3D printing. In addition, 102 (47 percent) offer 3D modeling, most likely with software such as SketchUp or Tinkercad (a computer-aided design tool). A final relevant category from the survey was prototyping, offered by 43 respondents (20 percent). Prototyping is defined as creating models of a product or solution that you hope to create but need to test first, and it can be done in ways other than 3D printing. Likewise, 3D printers are used for much more than prototyping. This chapter is likely the best place to make note of prototyping, since it is something that can be pursued in a makerspace and certainly done with 3D printing. Overall, 3D printing is widely available in library makerspaces, as shown by the survey results, and is likely to grow given the developments detailed here.

Making Possibilities

There are a multitude of making possibilities for your patrons beyond the short life of objects mentioned so far. Based on a page of results on the Yeggi.com design search engine, patrons could make an iPhone stand, a castle, a clock, a stamp, a safety razor, a BB-gun pellet trap, a wrench, a whistle, an aquaponics grow bed, a padlock with key, and on and on (see figure 9.2 for one example). None of these products might interest you, but you can always make something you would be interested in. It might be more useful, though, to talk about the different directions that patrons' 3D making could take. Think of these as categories of making that they could pursue. More of the how-to and design sources for 3D printing follow.

Prototyping

Makers could turn to the 3D printer with prototyping in mind. They could use the tools of 3D printing to create a model of a desired end product. They might be making it at a smaller size or out of a different type of material than the end product—and the final item might not be created with a 3D printer at all. The idea behind prototyping is to test a concept before you take the time to create something that might be more time-consuming or expensive to make. The 3D printer does the making for you, layer after layer, all for the cost of a little plastic.

Final Product

Alternatively, maybe the object created is the final product. It could be a stand-alone item that serves a purpose all by itself. It could be a solid piece, or it could contain moving parts. It could be a part of another whole item or maybe a missing piece. You may have broken a piece off of something, lost a game piece, or needed one more of those clips to get the shower curtain hanging right; now you could just print it out. Patrons could walk away with the completion of an existing item or a new beginning with something that stands alone.

Self-Designed Objects

3D print jobs can be printed from designs from a patron's own head—well, not directly, but through the mechanism of 3D design software (discussed in detail in the next section). An imagined item can be brought into digital existence on a computer and then transmitted into three-dimensionality with the 3D printer.

Figure 9.2. *Make:* magazine 3D printer shootout. *Image provided through a CC BY 2.0 License by John Abella (jabella), http://www.flickr.com/photos/jabella/9440443380.*

Other-Designed Objects

The printed 3D objects can also be items designed by someone else. This can be a very satisfying and relatively easy project for someone new to 3D printing: find a 3D item online and then print it out. It is a magical experience to hold something that you have previously seen only on the screen.

Crowdsourced Objects

As a cross between the prior two options, your patron might show her or his own talents by modifying an already existing design. This collaboration between a person in the flesh and one or more digital creators of an object leads to a final product that owes its existence to multiple authors. To further extend the path of this object, your patron might share the design online, where a larger crowd might continue its development.

◎ Understanding 3D Printing

3D printers create objects through a process known as additive layer manufacturing, in which successive layers of material are extruded out of the printer head to complete a design (Kim, 2017). Essentially, the object is made by applying multiple layers of material to a surface. 3D objects are thus built from the ground up; the item that you are printing grows taller as the material piles up. You can watch the printer lay down material in one area of your creation and then skip over others to allow for curves, holes, or markings in the item. The printer follows along its path, completing the needed material or skipping the laying down of the material in each zone of the object, until the design is complete and it can rest. This can be seen in part in figure 9.3.

The 3D printers that you will see in a library makerspace use plastic as their medium. The plastic filament, which can be any color or clear, needs to be melted by the printer to create the image. The filament is like a colorful piece of spaghetti, wound around a spool for storage, from which it is fed into the printer. It is possible to use multiple colors in 3D printing by changing out the filament partway into the job, but it is not possible to have colors alternate across each layer. You can make a statue that is red at the bottom and yellow on top. The plastic object can also be painted to allow for a more colorful result.

The two main types of plastic filament used in 3D printers are ABS (acrylonitrile butadiene styrene), which is made from petroleum, and PLA (polylactide), which is created from plants such as corn, sugarcane, or potatoes. PLA tends to be more pliable than ABS, which is both stronger and harder when set. These two plastics are certainly not the only two types of filaments readily used in today's 3D printers. Also used to create 3D objects are wood, bronze, ceramic, polyester, and many more (Kim, 2017).

3D printing is not a fast process. Depending on the size of the object and the thickness of the plastic or other material, the whole process can take anywhere from a few hours to a few days. This definitely influences expectations on being able to quickly produce items with this technology. Videos of 3D printers at work are exciting to watch, but you have to keep in mind that they generally compress time by quite a bit. It is crucial when planning workshops on 3D design and printing to remember that the participants will not be able to walk away with a finished product at the end of the hour. Library makerspaces with 3D printers have to set up processes for providing users with estimates on when printing jobs will complete.

Figure 9.3. Probibliot31. *Image provided through a CC BY 2.0 License by FryskLab, http://www. flickr.com/photos/83026924@N03/12464584064.*

⑥ Benefits of 3D Printing

Aside from the wow factor of 3D printing, what draws people to use it? What keeps people working on new printers and techniques? The folks at All That 3D (2017) offer a list of ten appealing aspects of 3D printing today and in the near future. The following are the eight that are most representative of current printing capacities in the library makerspace:

1. 3D printing is a more affordable method of prototyping than traditional machining.
2. 3D printed objects are quick to produce and results are seen fast.
3. 3D designs are easily customizable and do not cost more.
4. The main skill required for printing is to be able to create the design file rather than run the equipment.
5. The printer allows for intricate designs that are impossible for traditional machinery and methods.
6. Using diverse materials is easy and affordable.
7. 3D printing is environmentally friendly and energy efficient.
8. 3D printers are more accessible to consumers than traditional manufacturing machines.

The appeal of fashioning something out of nothing but an idea in your head is constant across different media of construction. There is something different in 3D printing, though, which combines the relatively low investments of skill and human effort with a very flexible piece of equipment to produce an extremely detailed outcome. Furthermore, not all parts of the 3D-printing process are simple to enact or are without room for failure in the design, the medium, or the equipment. What appears true about 3D printing is that as the equipment grows cheaper and more widely available, there is no shortage of makers continuing to join in and push the boundaries of this mode of creation.

⊚ Supplying for 3D Printing

3D printing makes it possible to imagine an object, design it on a computer, and then bring it into being. Therefore, the list of tools is quite small: a design file and a 3D printer. There are many choices of printers and methods for obtaining a design, however. This section of the chapter examines options among printers, sources for existing designs, software to use in creating new designs, and methods for scanning 3D objects.

3D Printers

For library makerspaces, 3D printers will tend to be consumer-oriented devices in the range of $2,500 or less. They all use a process known as FDM (fused deposition modeling) to create items, which involves the melting of plastic and the process of spreading layers described earlier. A useful list of printers and their characteristics is found in *PC Magazine*'s "The Best 3D Printers of 2017" (Hoffman, 2017), including current prices for the equipment. One sample printer is shown in figure 9.4. The printers come with software to transmit the 3D design file to the printer. As with many products, you tend to get what you pay for, with increased features or speed available in the more expensive models. Here are short synopses of three printers, which point out some of the choices that you have when selecting one.

MakerBot Replicator+

MakerBot is a very popular brand of 3D printers, with its devices featured in many of the makerspace profiles in this book and in the literature on library makerspaces. The Replicator+ (figure 9.1; see https://www.makerbot.com/replicator for more information) prints using PLA filament and costs around $2,300. It offers a larger maximum size for a printed object (11.6 × 7.6 × 6.5 inches) than the other two listed here. It also works a bit faster, depending on the object to be printed. MakerBot has been in the business for a long time and has a large community of users to draw on. It also created Thingiverse.com, a huge collection of 3D design files that can be printed on the MakerBot. So, the Replicator+ prints larger objects with lots of community support fairly quickly but is more expensive than the other two. If you would like the flexibility of larger items, it might be worth paying more up front.

Lulzbot Mini 3D Printer

Lulzbot's Mini 3D printer is a high-performance desktop printer that is sold at $1,250. While the build area may be smaller than the Replicator+ at 6 × 6 × 6.2 inches, this printer is incredibly easy to use and prints in more materials, including ABS, PLA, HIPS (high-impact polystyrene), PVA (polyvinyl alcohol), wood-filled filaments, polyester (Tritan), PETT (polyethylene co-trimethylene terephthalate), bronze- and copper-filled filaments, polycarbonate, nylon, PETG (glycol-modified polyethylene terephthalate), conductive PLA and ABS, UV luminescent filaments, nylon PCTPE (plasticized copolyamide TPE [thermoplastic elastomer]), PC-ABS (polycarbonate-acrylonitrile butadiene styrene), Alloy 910, and more every day. The Lulzbot Mini (figure 9.4; see https://www.lulzbot.com/store/printers/lulzbot-mini) also has the advantageous feature of automatically leveling the print bed each time it begins a new print job, so users don't need to

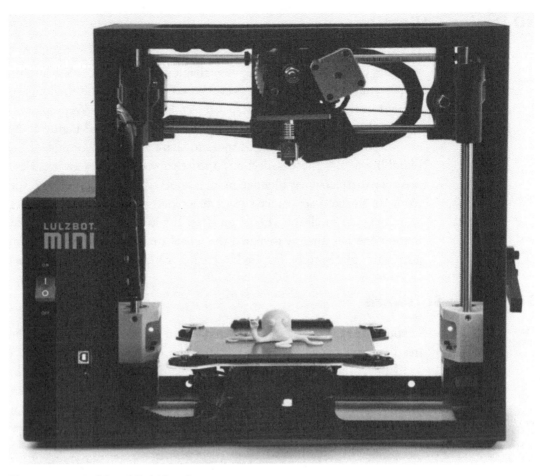

Figure 9.4. Lulzbot Mini 3D printer.

adjust it themselves. The author (Ellyssa) has owned a Lulzbot Mini for nearly two years and recommends it highly.

RepRap Mendel

Could you save money by building your own 3D printer? Yes, indeed! The RepRap project (http://reprap.org/wiki) offers free plans for creating a 3D printer for $600 or less. There are multiple models to choose from, with Mendel being just one. The Mendel (see http://reprap.org/wiki/Mendel) prints both PLA and ABS filament. It prints objects up to 8 × 8 × 5.5 inches—so a bit larger than the Lulzbot Mini and a bit smaller than the Replicator+. The speed of printing is closer to the Lulzbot than to the Replicator+. For this printer, you can pay less and get a larger maximum size item than the Lulzbot, while continuing to have flexibility in plastics. It is much cheaper than the Replicator+ and only slightly smaller in maximum size. The real question comes in your willingness to make a RepRap Mendel by yourself.

An interesting aspect of the project is that it is aimed toward making a self-replicating device so that many of the parts of the printer can be printed by another RepRap printer. So, you could reach out to a member of the RepRap community and see if someone would be willing to assist you in this process. As the wiki recommends, you have to be interested in not only 3D printing but also the journey of making such a printer.

3D Design Collections

When you are looking for something to print on your 3D printer, note that there is a growing collection of 3D designs available for anyone to access and print as is or to modify per your own wishes. Thingiverse.com has been around the longest and has the largest current collection. The RepRap Object Library (http://reprap.org/wiki/The_RepRap_Object_Library) has a small selection to draw from. YouMagine.com and Cubehero.com are relatively new additions as spots to share and locate designs. In attempting to make searching across these collections and other smaller ones easier, Blender 3D Model Repository (https://www.blender-models.com) shows results from all the object repositories from its site and serves as a place to upload your designs, while Yeggi.com serves as a search engine of all the 3D design sites. The idea here is that there are many places to see if someone has already invented the wheel that you were about to unknowingly reinvent and many places to be inspired to create or modify your own version for printing.

3D Design Software

If you cannot find an existing design for an object or if you need to modify one, you will need to turn to 3D design software. One of the most popular 3D design applications available is the free online computer-aided designed program Tinkercad. Tinkercad is an easy-to-use drafting program that lets users quickly create 3D designs by dragging and dropping shapes around its simple interface. No design experience is necessary to use this software, which is well loved by people of all ages. Figure 9.5 shows a Tinkercad tutorial.

Additionally, there are two more great applications to use, both of which have a free version. SketchUp (http://www.sketchup.com) has a Make version for free and a Pro version for purchase. It is available for both Windows and Mac. Blender (http://www.blender.org) is an open-source tool that meets a variety of 3D modeling needs in addition to 3D printing. It is available for download for Windows, Mac, and Linux.

3D Scanning

Another route to take toward creating a needed 3D design file is to use a 3D scanner or a related method. In fact, the 123D Catch app is a method of 3D scanning in that you can take a picture of an object or a person and have the app create a 3D file. You could also use a MakerBot Digitizer desktop 3D scanner https://www.amazon.com/gp/product/B00FOUCBOO?tag=ttr_3d-scanner-20), which can scan an object up to eight inches across and eight inches tall. You can also use an Xbox 360 Kinect for 3D scanning (a game controller that you operate by having it continuously scan your body); directions for doing so are available at http://www.instructables.com/id/EASY-Kinect-3D-Scanner/.

◎ Maintaining the Makerspace

For 3D printing, plastic will be the main refill needed. Many 3D printers come with a starter amount of filament, and it is helpful to note how quickly you use the filament for early testing and projects so that you can plan ahead and stock up. Other ongoing costs will be there for print maintenance and repair. The printer needs to be oiled on occasion, and some of its parts may wear out (for which you could potentially print replacements using the printer, assuming that a key part is not broken). Repairs of the printers are gen-

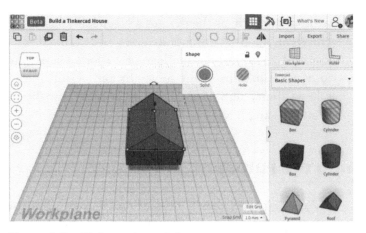

Figure 9.5. Tinkercad tutorial.

erally not difficult, but they do require the person making the repairs to be brave enough to open up the equipment and make needed adjustments.

Allocating Space

The good news is that 3D printers and scanners do not need much space to operate. However, you will want to provide enough room to work with items that you are scanning or to open up the printer to clean it out or make adjustments. You will also need space for a computer that will transmit the 3D design to the printer and control the printing. A very key element for 3D printers is ventilation as filaments can release varying levels of volatile organic compounds (VOCs) into the air as they are melted. ABS filament is considered toxic and nonbiodegradable, whereas PLA, being plant based, is nontoxic and biodegradable (Delecki, 2017). Therefore, you will want to position your 3D printer in a well-ventilated area or beside a window.

The printing process is not particularly messy, but facets of finishing a 3D printed object can be. Sometimes, there are extra pieces of plastic called supports that print while connected to the object to scaffold it and keep it from falling as the object prints. The supports are broken off or otherwise removed once the job completes; the object is then sanded to remove any remaining support material.

Two last space-related issues are important to consider. One is providing enough space in the makerspace or the library to store the plastic that you will use. The other is to think ahead from your first 3D printer to where you might put the second, third, fourth, or fifth printers if you build your service.

Considering Intellectual Property

Intellectual property will be an important concern when dealing with 3D printing as it allows you to create 3D objects of anything that you can scan or design. While this is a topic that all makerspaces should cover, library makerspaces are very well situated to talk about intellectual property concerns. Your library's mission typically contains a role or responsibility to be aware and give guidance in copyright and fair use provisions and questions. With the open-source collections of designs, the resulting objects can be printed without concern, as the designs are generally shared under Creative Commons licensing. However, if a patron wants to scan a trademarked action figure or design something that looks an awful lot like the logo of a sports team, caution is needed. Libraries will want to educate patrons about copyright and personal use versus creating items for sale. The role of library staff in a makerspace is to help makers build their understanding of these situations and navigate them as they arise.

Envisioning the Future of 3D Printing

3D printers have already become much more affordable and user friendly for the average consumer. They can even be purchased at electronics stores such as Best Buy and wholesale grocery stores such as Sam's Club for less than $300 for models such as the XYZ-printing da Vinci Mini. And 3D printing pens can be had for between $50 and $100.

There are also 3D printers that will print out food, such as the Pancake Bot, affordable at less than $300 (see http://www.pancakebot.com), and many more are currently in development. The near future will likely see many more 3D printers capable of printing food items such as the Mmuse Desktop Chocolate 3D Printer and the still-in-development Foodini from Natural Machines. This trend is so popular that there is an annual 3D Foodprinting Conference that takes place in the Netherlands each summer.

Specialty filaments are another growth area for this industry with new materials continually being readied for 3D printing. Already there is a glow-in-the dark filament available, a color changing filament, a coffee-filled filament, and even filaments filled with beer and hemp, as well as a wide range of metals and wood.

And 3D printing start-ups that specialize in 3D printing niche items such as jewelry, footwear, personalized action figures, medical supplies, and more have launched. Made in Space has developed a zero-gravity 3D printer and will even print your parts "off world" for you.

With all this considered, there are some very interesting times ahead for making physical items with 3D printers of all sorts.

Library Makerspace Profile: DeLaMare Science and Engineering Library, University of Nevada, Reno, NV

https://guides.library.unr.edu/making-resources

Tara Radniecki, Engineering Librarian, DeLaMare Science and Engineering Library

How Did Your Makerspace Come to Be?

The makerspace in the DeLaMare Science and Engineering Library grew organically out of an effort to revitalize and reconnect the STEM-focused library to its target population on campus. Knowing that faculty and students in the sciences and engineering tend to favor collaborative and flexible work spaces, the library took out stacks of unused materials (sending them to an on-site automated storage retrieval system), brought in large tables for group work, and painted the walls with whiteboard paint. The library had been checking out headphones to use in the library and expanded its lending technology collection to include other items that facilitate learning and innovation outside the classroom, including graphing calculators, SparkFun Arduino Inventor Kits, and soldering irons. As the library once again became popular with students and faculty, the chemistry department approached the library in 2012 about acquiring a 3D printer to aid in teaching and research. Two 3D printers were initially purchased (one hobbyist level and one higher end) and saw significant use from the beginning. It was clear the impact such innovative technologies could have on users in the sciences and engineering as 3D printed molecules allowed students to learn in new ways and students created items that had never existed before. Having no dedicated budget, the makerspace continued to grow through targeted partnerships on campus for larger, more expensive items. The Office of Research and Innovation and the engineering departments funded the acquisition of an additional 3D printer, 2 Artec 3D scanners, a PCB (printed circuit board) milling machine, and a laser cutter. These partners knew that having such equipment live in a library instead of individual labs allows everyone to access them and facilitates innovation at a much bigger scale across the entire campus. The library has been able to fund increases to the lending technology collection, which now includes two HTC Vives, Oculus Rifts, and other virtual reality apparatuses; Leap Motion sensors, Raspberry Pis, LEGO Mindstorms robotic kits, tools, button makers, Geiger counters, and other items needed for innovation, making, and learning.

Who Uses It?

The majority of our users are undergraduate students in the STEAM disciplines. Engineering students regularly use the space to work on assigned projects in a wide array of classes and on side projects and entrepreneurial endeavors. Those in the sciences, including chemistry, biology, psychology, and anthropology, also regularly use the space for creating unique labware and research apparatuses, and for 3D scanning. The addition of a laser and vinyl cutter brought in many new users from the arts community and several classes now require their students to use the space in creating projects. 3D scanners, 3D printers, and Tech Wrangler consultations have brought in local artists looking to create large-scale works for Burning Man and to create digital files of their existing work. While most users are students, faculty, and staff from the university, many community members have come to use the equipment and other makerspace services. Several local start-ups in the region prototyped their designs in the DeLaMare Library makerspace and local economic authorities and entrepreneurial support service groups regularly point community members to our freely available services and resources.

How Do You Market the Makerspace?

No formal marketing strategy has been implemented for the makerspace. The available equipment and consultation services can be found on the homepage of the library's website. Liaison librarians talk about the space when doing their regular outreach and instruction in the classroom, with student groups, in faculty meetings, or other on-campus avenues. The library regularly hosts K–12 groups and conducts tours of the makerspace, encouraging attendees to come back and use the space. Multiple times each year the library also goes out and does outreach events, demoing makerspace equipment and services at K–12 events; entrepreneurial-focused events; start-up, art, and maker faires; and many other events where community members can learn about the resources and services. Most of the users learn about the space through word of mouth. The library has been able to create a network of partnerships both on and off campus that have allowed those looking for these services to find them through referrals.

Who Supports It?

The makerspace is completely integrated into the library as a whole. Therefore, all members of the staff, both full-time and student employees, support users in the space. Each employee is trained on processing 3D print jobs, helping users with the laser and vinyl cutters, checking out lending technologies, and helping with other services provided in the space. The library also trains two to four student employees to be Tech Wranglers. These Tech Wranglers acquire a high level of knowledge in 3D modeling, 3D scanning, laser cutting, PCB milling, and all the other offerings in the makerspace. They are the staff experts and also conduct one-on-one consultations with users on any projects using equipment in the makerspace. Tech Wranglers are available approximately twenty to thirty hours each week, a relatively small portion of the library's total opening time. This is why each staff member must be able to assist with the majority of services in the space at any given time.

What Does It Include?

The DeLaMare Science and Engineering Library houses the following equipment:

- 3D printing and 3D scanning
  - Stratasys SE Plus 3D printer
  - Z Printer (plaster-based 3D printer)
  - Sintratec Kit SLS 3D printer
  - Artec Eva and Spider 3D Scanners
- Epilog 75-watt laser cutter
- Large-format vinyl cutter
- Heat press (primarily for heat transfer vinyl)
- LPKF PCB milling machine
- Soldering bar (stocked with various irons, tools, solder)
- Sewing bar (stocked with sewing machine, needles, threads)
- Virtual reality
  - HTC Vive
  - Oculus Rift
  - Google Glass
  - VR One
- Programmables (or items that can be developed for)
  - Makey Makey kits
  - Sparkfun Arduino Inventor Kits
  - LEGO Mindstorm robotic kits
  - Raspberry Pis
  - Leap Motion sensor
  - Apple Watch
- Circuit Scribe
- Geiger counter

- Various hand tools, drills, soldering irons
- Button maker

The library also has the following available for consultations:

- Tech Wranglers: http://unr.libcal.com/booking/techwranglers
- Photoshop: http://unr.libcal.com/booking/photoshop
- Patents and trademarks: http://unr.libcal.com/appointments/?g=677

How Do You Stay Aware of Developments in Makerspaces?

Members of the library are very active professionally. They attend conferences, collaborate with librarians at other institutions on makerspaces, and keep abreast of the literature, both scholarly and popular. They also work closely with other local makerspaces, coworking spaces, and entrepreneurial-supporting groups in the region and learn from each other.

What Do You See Happening in Your Makerspace in the Next Year?

The DeLaMare Library makerspace is continually providing access to new resources and services in order to meet the needs of the user population. It will be acquiring more virtual reality sets (HTV Vive) to accommodate the growing interest in the College of Engineering. It is experimenting with different types of 3D printers and filaments to help meet user needs in prototyping new knowledge objects. It will also be working to expand its popular consultation service to include more topics and with more time availability.

What Is Your Advice to Others Who Would Like to Create a Makerspace?

First, start talking to your target population and gaging their interest. They are probably already aware of some of the more common makerspace offerings such as 3D printing. Ask them what they would like to utilize or learn more about. Ask them what they would love to try to make if they had the funds and/or access to equipment to do so. Since there are so many makerspaces currently out there serving a wide variety of populations, talk to those who run the makerspaces and see how they serve their populations in order to find out what makes sense in trying to meet your community's needs.

Focus as much on teaching the skills necessary to use the equipment as you do on simply providing access to the machines. A makerspace is only as impactful as its users are knowledgeable in using it. Be aware of all the new skills users will need and find ways to provide opportunities and avenues for them to acquire and learn them.

Create a network of partners. No makerspace can provide all the resources every person may need. Seek out the other spaces in your region in order to learn what the other has and to collaboratively build makerspace collections together. In a smaller city, you may not need to have a PCB milling machine in your makerspace if another already provides access to one. By filling in existing gaps in resources in the community, your budget can also go further in providing unique resources and driving new users to the library. Make sure you approach prospective partners outside of makerspaces as well. Seek out organizations and companies that support innovation and entrepreneurship to see how a library makerspace might help them and their users. Approach local K–12 schools to see if there are opportunities to work together to bring makerspace experiences to students both in and outside the classroom.

⊚ Library Makerspace Profile: ACU Maker Lab, Abilene Christian University Library, Abilene, TX

http://blogs.acu.edu/makerlab

Laura Baker, Librarian for Digital Research and Learning, Abilene Christian University Library

How Did Your Makerspace Come to Be?

In 2012, the dean of libraries at Abilene Christian University (ACU), Dr. John Weaver, began exploring the role of creativity in education. He identified digital fabrication, design thinking, and the Internet of Things as new realities that would affect students' futures. Such design skills were closely connected to the maker movement and the do-it-yourself initiatives that were becoming so popular, but Weaver also saw them connected to the mission of libraries. He began conducting conversations to explore how the ACU Library could be part of preparing students for that future. How can creativity, deliberate prototyping, and community-shared resources be used as pedagogical tools that fuel learning?

After staff visited a number of makerspaces in large urban areas, the ACU Library created a short documentary to introduce the campus to the values of making. The video, called "We Are Makers," contains interviews with people at *Make:* magazine, Etsy, and other high-profile creativity centers, all reflecting on the cross-disciplinary skills that making inspires and develops. The video helped key decision makers on campus, as well as people within the library, see the potential that a makerspace could have on a university campus.

At the same time, ACU was ramping up educational programs in science and engineering, departments with a natural interest in maker technology. The library was going to reclaim some space from another campus office that had been in the library building but that would now be moving elsewhere, so the time seemed right to set up the Maker Lab. With funding from the university provost and the library's own budget, the ACU Library Maker Lab doors opened in 2013.

Who Uses It?

The Maker Lab is open to all students, staff, and faculty at ACU regardless of major and even to anyone from the community regardless of whether they are affiliated with the university. Children are welcome provided they are accompanied by parents as appropriate.

A large portion of ACU makers are art and design students and some engineering students. There are also informal student groups interested in coding, robotics, or gaming. However, the majority of people who use the Maker Lab are those who simply are pursuing a personal need or interest. They want to make something and heard about this cool place in the library where they can do that. They learn to make artwork on the laser cutter, embroider gifts for friends, and make something unique on the 3D printer.

As the space has grown, many children from area schools use it. Homeschool groups learn 3D design on their own and come to the Maker Lab to print their creations. Schools bring students for field trips as a reward for accomplishing reading goals, and in the summer, the library hosts short Maker Academy camps for kids and middle schoolers. The school connections are the Maker Lab's fastest growing group of users.

How Do You Market the Space?

Ongoing marketing activities include the Maker Lab's website, having interactive displays on the library's main floor, and informal talks with professors about how to integrate the Maker Lab into their teaching. The Maker Lab also asks people who come to the Maker Lab to sign in by swiping an ID. This lets the lab create an e-mail list of visitors to inform them of special events and news items. The ACU Library and Maker Lab are part of campus tours for prospective students and their parents, giving the space additional exposure.

In addition to the small, ongoing activities described earlier, the Maker Lab hosts two intense events. One is a campus Maker Fest. Maker Fest is where people demonstrate the projects they have made and how they made them. There are tool demonstrations, exhibitions, food, and hands-on activities for people of all ages, all in an informal carnival-like atmosphere. Area makers and schools are invited. Over six hundred visitors showed up at the last Maker Fest.

The second big event is the series of Maker Academy camps hosted during the summer. The elementary kids camps are two days, and the middle school camps are three days. Fliers and e-mails advertise the camps to area schools and university parents. As the camps have been successful, word of mouth helps spread the news.

Who Supports It?

There is a full-time manager hired specifically to run the daily operations of the Maker Lab, to supervise the student workers, and to monitor what goes on. The executive director is a professor from the campus art department and is supported in the Maker Lab with a stipend. These two report to the head of educational technology, who reports to the dean of libraries.

One librarian works several days a week in the Maker Lab as an add-on to regular librarian duties. This librarian also serves on the Maker Lab council that plans activities and conducts other administrative matters. Having a librarian actively involved in the Maker Lab and its oversight helps integrate the space with the rest of the library.

What Does It Include?

The most popular tool is a laser cutter with an 18 x 24-inch bed. There are three plastic filament 3D printers, including one that the lab manager built from a kit. There is also a resin printer for finer 3D printing. The fiber arts center has three sewing machines, a serger, and an embroidery machine, with assorted threads, sewing needles, crochet hooks, and other notions. The woodworking area has a CNC (computer numerical control) router, band saw, table saw, planer, miter saw, belt sander, and numerous hand tools. All sections include scrap material for free to encourage people to try new ideas. If makers require material other than what is available as free scrap, they buy and bring it themselves. Limited supplies, like big sheets of plywood, are available to buy from the Maker Lab.

A classroom area with individual tables seats approximately twenty-four people. White boards, work tables, and storage bins for small projects allow room to work. Three desktop computers are reserved for design work.

How Do You Stay Aware of Developments in Makerspaces?

The Maker Lab manager and the executive director both try to attend Maker Faire in New York. This event and its accompanying videos posted on YouTube are primary sources of information about tools and ideas for new projects. *Make:* is a magazine offering project ideas and guidance for makerspaces. The maker librarian also attends library conferences and participates in listservs such as LITA-L for ongoing discussions related to making in libraries.

What Do You See Happening in Your Makerspace in the Next Year?

Adding another laser cutter and more computers is on the list of priorities. Part of the Maker Lab space is regularly used as a classroom by the engineering department, but they will no longer need this space next semester. The Maker Lab hopes to reclaim that space to expand its work area. ACU Library will be seeking a private grant to support the development of an entrepreneurial center where groups can take their ideas beyond the making stage into fuller implementation. The library would like to support more projects aligned with making for social good and that address real world problems rather than simply personal interests. This will require stronger partnerships with classes on campus and with development centers connected with the city.

What Is Your Advice to Others Who Would Like to Create a Makerspace?

If the makerspace is for an academic campus or university, the library must connect making with learning. Popularity and attendance at events are partial indicators of success, but alone they are not enough. To make your space truly compelling, try to demonstrate the potential for real-world applications and solutions that it can offer. Show how small projects impart larger learning skills that makers can apply to other issues. Partnering with other entities—like city development departments, civic clubs, and area high schools that feed into the university—is a good way of building social capital that the university administration values.

On a practical level, don't be afraid to start small. Even a few pieces of equipment can go a long way. Look at community needs both on your campus and in your community. What clubs are active? What ages? Are there local people who have skills who could teach a workshop or be a maker-in-residence? Let that small start touch some major needs, and then grow the idea based on feedback.

⊚ Key Points

3D printing offers a unique creative realm to makers in a library makerspace. It should be seen as more than a fad, with the ability to create practical items.

- 3D printers enable patrons to create physical items from a digital design.
- A wide selection of 3D printers and design software is available, as well as many open collections of designs that can be printed as is or modified.
- 3D printing puts the creation of items in the hands of the maker and may expand to print in plastic and metal.

Now on to some unexpected types of making that library makerspaces are pursuing.

⊚ References

All That 3D. 2017. "10 Insane Benefits of 3D Printing." https://www.allthat3d.com/3d-print-ing-benefits.

Delecki, Kevin. 2017. "Safety and Guidelines in the Library Makerspace." In *The Makerspace Librarian's Sourcebook*, edited by Ellyssa Kroski, 73–84. Chicago: American Library Association.

Hoffman, Tony. 2017. "The Best 3D Printers of 2017." *PC Magazine*. http://www.pcmag.com/article2/0,2817,2470038,00.asp.

Kim, Bohyun. 2017. "A Librarian's Guide to 3D Printing." In *The Makerspace Librarian's Sourcebook*, edited by Ellyssa Kroski, 87–112. Chicago: American Library Association.

CHAPTER 10

Resources for the Unexpected

Lesser-Known Making

NOT ALL MAKING IS WHAT YOU WOULD imagine as many have devised alternative activities to provide some variety for seasoned makers, and others have developed outreach activities to draw in novices. One might not consider the culinary arts as a maker interest, but cooking is an activity found in many makerspaces and kitchen tool libraries are located all over the United States. Gardening and composting are examples of green making and not likely activities that one would think to find in a library makerspace, yet they are. These and other unexpected maker activities will be discussed in this chapter along with their adoption in library makerspaces.

Making Possibilities

The next examples of making are each unique, although there is a bit of a thread in the first few. It is similar to the items in the earlier chapters, but there are fewer shared pieces of equipment or space requirements for them. The "Refills Needed" and "Special Space Requirements" sections that are part of the preceding chapter are missing from this one, and the tools involved in each form of making are briefly mentioned within their descriptions rather than being separated out. Again, as you read these, consider that these making activities have all taken place in a library and continue to take place. Maybe they will soon be in your library.

Bricks and Beer

The Bricks and Beer outreach program hosted by the Fort Vancouver Regional Library District, Washington, presents an opportunity for "adult fans of LEGO bricks to gather at a local restaurant to create, share ideas and enjoy a beer together." This innovative program was launched with the hope of introducing new people to the library and letting them know that the library is not just for reading but also for creativity, idea sharing, and fun. By meeting in a familiar place that potential patrons already frequent, this program not only provides them with a unique maker activity, but builds relationships between the library and local restaurants and businesses which sell LEGO bricks (Urban Libraries Council, 2016a).

Repair Cafe

Fort Vancouver Regional Library District, Washington, hosts a Repair Cafe in which patrons bring in broken appliances, clothing, and electronics to have them repaired by volunteers. Patrons with broken items sit across from volunteer fixers in hopes of building community. This event attracted new patrons who had never before been to the library, as well as those who enjoy tinkering and the challenge of repairing items, and was so popular that it has become a regular part of the library's programming (Urban Libraries Council, 2016c).

Tinkering

Tinkering is an activity that a library makerspace can enable, but it is a hard one to clearly define in terms of process, required equipment, or replacement items. For all the structure that there is in people's lives and educational experiences, there is something valuable in activities that operate by the rules of serendipity. Tinkering is the process of making small changes to an object in order to improve or repair it. In the context of an educational activity, tinkering offers learners the opportunity for problem solving through hands-on projects (The Exploratory, 2015). It is something that you can intentionally pursue as a way to inspire makers; it is also a natural response that people will have to new technologies.

The informal survey of library makerspaces revealed that ninety-five respondents (43 percent) support tinkering as an activity. This is likely to involve use of items in the makerspace that have other intended purposes. Whether library patrons are children or adults, having an array of resources to work with can allow them to test out making activities or combine various items as needed to solve a problem or make something that interests them. This free-flowing approach to learning is going to be a part of any makerspace, with only the tools available differing. Probably the most useful approach to equipping a library makerspace for tinkering is to have a variety of types of making represented. The interplay of materials can open up people's imaginations and allow tinkering to thrive.

Tinkering might lead into something a bit more defined, such as some of the other areas included on the survey—for example, bicycle building/maintenance (three respondents, or 1 percent). There are certainly tinkering aspects to working in this area, trying out different solutions to problems with bicycles. Or, tinkering might lead to practice with making materials and equipment that builds skill and creates a fluid mind that can be applied to various areas.

Minecraft

Minecraft might at first seem like more of an entry in a book on game playing in libraries rather than making in libraries. It certainly deserves a place there as a very popular online and mobile app game. The key element in this game is the making that happens—from small acts, such as digging tunnels as a defensive maneuver, to immense building efforts that re-create parts of one's world within the Minecraft world (see one example in figure 10.1). By providing physical space and server space to host Minecraft activities, libraries can support and encourage the creativity that Minecraft players display. This creativity develops players' knowledge and skills in spatial relations, planning, mathematics, and understanding the capacities of the materials and equipment used to build items in the games. "Minecraft inserts players into a geometric environment in which they must exercise spatial awareness and reasoning to effectively interact with the environment of the game" (Hultstrand, 2015).

Libraries can set up their own Minecraft server to let patrons come to the library and play Minecraft together. This is an example of providing easy access to the game for collaborative building efforts and adventures. It is also possible to turn interest in the game into related making activities such as creating paper crafts and 3D-printed items, and working with circuits. Minecraft has also inspired library makers to create items to control game movement using Makey Makeys.

Figure 10.1. Minecraft Ottawa map. *Image provided through a CC BY 2.0 License by Richard Akerman, https://www.flickr.com/photos/rakerman/24642200002/.*

Seed Libraries and Green Making

It is possible that another practical area might be ripe for makerspace program development: activities related to gardening, composting, and even farming. There is some evidence that this is a growing area for makers. But enough puns—here are some examples that other libraries could build on. The Pima County Public Library in Tucson, Arizona, operates a seed library from which patrons can borrow seeds, with the hope that they will have a good growing experience and can return seeds from their own plants to the library. More information is available at https://www.library.pima.gov/seed-library, including a list of additional seed libraries across the country. In 2015, the Seed Library of Pima County Public Library hosted the first-ever International Seed Library Forum. This innovative event was organized around the concept of food security and sustainability. "Over four days, attendees from seven countries participated in table discussions, author talks, seed swaps, poetry readings, and documentary viewings" (Urban Libraries Council, 2016b).

Composting is a very environmentally friendly activity that consists of letting natural items decompose rather than fill up landfills. Holding composting workshops can guide patrons in making their own compost bins such as the one offered by the Northbrook Public Library (Illinois). This is certainly a creative act that can revitalize soil and help create more items to enjoy and then compost. This idea of working the land as a form of making has an even more compelling example in the creation of the Library Idea Farm makerspace in Old Bridge, New Jersey (Old Bridge Public Library, 2017). The library has created a combination workshop and demonstration garden to combine 3D printing, sewing, gardening, and other maker activities. See more information here: http://www.oldbridgelibrary.org/resources/idea-farm.

Tool Libraries

Moving into more general tools than just kitchen items, there are a number of membership-based tool-lending libraries. They lend items such as concrete saws, tile cutters, and lawn mowers for an annual fee. There is a directory and map of more than eighty tool libraries in North America at http://localtools.org/find/. This could be an approach that libraries could learn from and take on tool lending as a service. The Oakland Public Library (California) has offered a growing tool library since 1991 and has an extensive list of tools and explanation of its policies at http://www.oaklandlibrary.org/locations/tool-lending-library. This again might be a natural outgrowth for a library makerspace—to offer access to equipment within the makerspace itself and then lend out other items for people to use at home.

Cooking

Cooking has a long history in libraries. There are many ways and reasons to connect your patrons with food and cooking in the library. You might have talented chefs come and demonstrate their cooking, or you might teach kids how to cook or have cooking classes for adults. In the informal survey of library makerspaces, 12 of the 219 respondents (5.5 percent) indicated that they provided food or culinary arts activities. It is unknown whether the cooking programs connected with these makerspaces predated the creation of the makerspace or were new additions to the library. Regardless, cooking can be a great

Figure 10.2. The new stand mixer. *Image provided through a CC BY 2.0 License by sylvar, http://www.flickr.com/photos/sylvar/76605024.*

opportunity to draw people in (everyone loves food!) and teach them something creative that they can pursue in the makerspace or at home. It would be interesting to see if libraries might add microwaves, ovens, and freezers in the same way that they are adding laser cutters and 3D printers.

Kitchen Tool Libraries

Some libraries have taken steps in that direction but with home use of equipment in mind rather than in-library activities. Libraries have typically provided communities with a common store of items to help people access materials that they cannot afford. Those who staff library makerspaces, as noted earlier in the book, have kept this same idea in mind with the technologies and activities that they offer. Types of equipment that libraries can offer are kitchen appliances and other tools. There are several kitchen tool libraries throughout the United States that can be located using the aforementioned Tool Lending Library Directory; examples include the Hub Tool Share, a lending library of gardening and cooking tools located in Bloomington, Indiana, and Kitchen Share NE, a public lending library for kitchen tools ranging from canning equipment to ice-cream makers in Portland, Oregon. The items may be too expensive for someone to buy for occasional use or two bulky to easily store, especially in a smaller kitchen (see examples in figure 10.2). Libraries are well suited to store and lend all sorts of materials and equipment, so why not small appliances? It would be interesting to tie lending the means of cooking into makerspace programming on cooking.

Button Maker

A creative activity that libraries may already engage in is button making. All that it takes is a button maker (sized for the button you would like to create), the top and bottom of the button (with pin or magnet), a plastic cover, and a paper circle with your image or words. It is very easy to create a template for a button design, as many have done and freely make available online. Once you have the template, it is a simple process to create buttons for patrons or have them choose their own messages or pictures and create their own. This is an easy and affordable addition to any library and perhaps the start of more making activities. Button maker machines can be had for less than $300 from companies such as American Button Machines and Tecre (the latter is highly recommended by author Ellyssa).

EggBot

A combination of robot and artistic device, the EggBot did not quite fit into chapters 7 or 8, and so here it sits in chapter 10. The EggBot can draw with a pen on spheres or egg-shaped items up to the size of a small grapefruit (see figure 10.3). It is programmed with Inkscape software, which allows you to digitally sketch a design that can then be drawn on the object. With a computer, Inkscape software, and the EggBot, you are ready to create some incredibly artistic eggs, ping-pong balls, or other items. You can use one color at a time, but for a multicolored result, you can switch pens out after each layer of your design is drawn. EggBots are an interesting addition to makerspaces because they

Figure 10.3. Eggbot at Cal Expo 21. *Image provided through a CC BY 2.0 License by Windell Oskay (oskay), http://www.flickr.com/photos/oskay/4820284466.*

combine multiple actions all in one place: do some programming, watch a robot draw, and walk away with a piece of art. More information and kits are available at http://egg-bot.com.

⊚ Library Makerspace Profile: LibLab: Makerspace and Technology Learning Center at South San Francisco Public Library, San Francisco, CA

http://www.ssfmakers.wordpress.com

Melisa Mendoza, Librarian I, South San Francisco Public Library

How Did Your Makerspace Come to Be?

The makerspace was spearheaded by a small team of administrators who rose to the challenge of creating relevant spaces for the community. Considering South San Francisco's history as "the Industrial City," they figured placing a wire-bending machine next to the book stacks wouldn't raise too many eyebrows. In 2014, the makerspace began as a small collection of equipment with irregular programming, inspired by Maker Faire in nearby San Mateo and libraries throughout the Bay Area. After several years of tinkering, LibLab has grown into its own dedicated space at both the main and branch library. Many thanks are owed two local companies who have helped fund acquisition of 3D printers, CNC (computer numerical control) machines, robots, and many other educational resources.

Who Uses It?

The LibLab Makerspace and Technology Learning Center is open to all ages with something for everyone. Grade school children visit after school to learn about robotics and programming. High school students create buttons as marketing materials for student council elections. College students use 3D printers for civil engineering projects that require prototyping. Elderly patrons come in to gain digital literacy with new laptops and cell phones, and to learn more about wearable health devices offered for circulation including Fitbits and blood pressure monitors.

There is also an active multigenerational sewing group that meets regularly to start on new projects and introduce the art of sewing to younger family members. The makerspace at South San Francisco Public Library creates a welcoming atmosphere to all of its multilingual and family-oriented patron base.

How Do You Market the Makerspace?

Local outreach has been a big part of letting the community know they have a free makerspace to use at their convenience. Staff promotes the makerspace by visiting elementary, middle, and high schools to create word-of-mouth recommendations from students to their families and friends. The branch library is located in the city downtown area where partnerships with local businesses create excitement about the buzzword *makerspace* and draws visitors to the library. Online marketing has been the most effective method of reaching new makerspace users. Therefore, the South San Francisco Public Library remains active across seven different social media platforms as well as the city website.

Who Supports It?

The makerspace is supported by the city of South San Francisco, by the Friends of South San Francisco Public Library, and through generous grants from Ms. Gladys Callan of Callan Realty, Sares Regis Community, and Education Fund and Devcon Construction, Inc.

What Does It Include?

As of May 2017, the makerspaces include various equipment for learning. In the area of science, there are three Ultimaker 3D printers, Squishy Circuit sets, Snap Circuit kits, Makey Makey modules, littleBits Gizmo and Gadgets, and Cubelets. For designing with technology there are Adobe Ink and Slide sets with fifteen available iPads, several 3Doodler pens, two Pancake Bots, a green screen, a 3D digital scanner, thirty laptops with designer software, and a Collaboration Room that includes a sixty-five-inch TV with a webcam, color printer, and computer loaded with Adobe Creative Suite products. For the builders and aspiring engineers there are LEGOs, Gears! Gears! Gears!, Roominate sets, GoldieBlox kits, and soldering irons available with helping hands. Crafters can get creative with two of the library's button makers, Silhouette Cameo paper crafting machine, DIWire rod bending machine, Othermill CNC machine, or the embroidery machine and sewing machines that come accompanied by an ironing board, cutting mats, and materials. Young programmers can learn through play with Dash and Dot robots, LEGO EV3 Mindstorms, two Meccanoid robots, Robot Turtles board game, and Arduino units that come with breadboards and wiring.

Besides all of this wonderful equipment, there is also a Self-Health Center that promotes healthy lifestyles through the availability of the Wearables for Wellness collection. The devices in this collection include the majority of Fitbit models, Garmin VivoActive HR, Jawbone UP3, LeapBand, Microsoft Band 2, Moov Now, Polar A360, TomTom Touch, GoPro Hero Session, Spire, Lumo Lift, Upright Posture Trainer, Garmin Index Smart Scale, Withings Smart Kid Scale, Withings Adult Digital Scale, and Withings Blood Pressure Monitor.

The final component of the makerspace includes the library's Tech Drop-In service, which allows patrons to bring in any technology-related questions from using new laptops, cell phones, or the Wearables for Wellness Collection. All of the makerspace equipment and services are completely free to the public.

How Do You Stay Aware of Developments in Makerspaces?

Being located in northern California and near Silicon Valley has its advantages. Some patrons are from the tech industry and willing to share news or insights. Also, much of the staff is involved with online networking with Bay Area STEM educators and other city libraries with makerspaces that share makerspace news, host local STEM meet-ups, and promote upcoming online webinars. Staff also attend the Bay Area Maker Faire as another great way to keep involved with new developments related to makerspaces.

What Do You See Happening in Your Makerspace in the Next Year?

The next year will be an exciting one as the library will have well-established procedures and policies in place with a growing team of dedicated staff. Much of the groundwork and planning should be finished within the next year. The team will then be able to shift focus to creating even more opportunities to connect with the diverse communities through STEAM programming and digital literacy workshops.

The summer months will be busy with park and recreation camp visits to the makerspace and extended makerspace hours at both the main and branch locations. When school is back in session, school visits and outreach will start back up. New equipment will arrive and the promotional efforts of staff will be revealed as program attendance is assessed. Virtual reality, augmented reality, 360 video, robotics, soldering, and music are possible areas for makerspace growth.

What Is Your Advice to Others Who Would Like to Create a Makerspace?

Planning is the biggest component of starting a makerspace. Ensuring that there is enough square footage for equipment, electrical outlets, workspace for patrons, storage of materials, and training for dedicated staff should be considered first before purchasing the latest and greatest equipment. Open-source software is great because a lot of it is free! Also, accepting LEGOs, cardboard, or other crafting materials as donations from patrons, local schools, and businesses is a great way to ease financial tension while building stronger community bonds.

⊚ Library Makerspace Profile: Maker Lab, Chicago Public Library, Chicago, IL

http://www.chipublib.org/maker-lab

Mark Andersen, Director of Learning and Economic Advancement, Chicago Public Library

How Did Your Makerspace Come to Be?

In the spring of 2012, a cadre of Chicago Public Library staff began touring incubators, accelerators, and digital media labs, and reading up on global libraries, adding new services that facilitated content creation among users.

In the fall, the Chicago Public Library Foundation applied for a grant through the Institute of Museums and Library Services (IMLS), which allowed the library to obtain equipment, renovate and update an underutilized space, and engage with users and the maker community in an impactful way.

The Maker Lab is led by the director of learning and economic advancement, Mark Andersen.

Who Uses It?

At the Chicago Public Library, staff believe in nurturing learning for all ages, and they support this by designing programs and services to develop and explore twenty-first-century skills.

Users who develop their skills at the Maker Lab are of all ages, but the majority of workshop attendees are aged eighteen to thirty-five. Users from teenagers to retirees participate in workshops and use the lab during designated "open shop" times when users work on personal projects that range from prototypes to gifts.

How Do You Market the Makerspace?

The Maker Lab is marketed on social media by the library's marketing team and the hashtag #cplmakerlab; by the Maker Lab Flickr stream; by e-mail in a monthly What's Happening at CPL e-blast; in print with a postcard, a Year of Making bookmark, and quarter-sheet fliers with our short links; and on MakersinChicago.org, a tool brought about through regular summits with our community maker partners.

Andersen markets the Maker Lab as an on-ramp to learning how to use 3D modeling and 2D design software for fabrication, and to discovering Chicago's growing maker ecosystem. It is a place for the graduates of our teen digital media spaces to test out, for creatives to try new technologies, and for the curious to keep learning.

Who Supports It?

The Maker Lab, initially supported by the IMLS grant, has since been supported by the Chicago Public Library Foundation, with funding by Motorola Mobility Foundation.

What Does It Include?

The lab contains four FDM (fused deposition modeling) 3D printers, two 40-watt laser cutters, one Carvey Desktop Mill, two electronic cutters, and laptops loaded with open-source and free software. The lab inherited a large projection screen, which aids in teaching workshops. Five two-seat work stations line one wall, and four tables sit in the center, around which hands-on crafting workshops take place.

How Do You Stay Aware of Developments in Makerspaces?

The Maker Lab team consists of information professionals and creative professionals who are eager to help newcomers experience the lab, and to learn from experienced makers, in person and online. This passion for learning and sharing has helped the lab experiment with different types of equipment and stay current with developments in the local entrepreneurial maker community.

What Do You See Happening in Your Makerspace in the Next Year?

The learnings so far indicate that users enjoy access to the technology and techniques. Some potential areas of exploration include engaging the community in new tool or workshop selection; installing regular artists-in-residence to inspire users; and literally branching out to other locations to engage the community in co-designing a makerspace.

What Is Your Advice to Others Who Would Like to Create a Makerspace?

The opportunity to learn alongside patrons is enriching for both the user and the staff. Library staff by necessity expand their learning and their understanding of learning, and exercise facilitation skills in every interaction. The collaborative learning is rewarding and can be applied to so many activities, tools, and technologies—a makerspace is not about what is in it; it is about the process, so do not be discouraged with a small budget.

◎ Key Points

Be open to all kinds of making that could appear in your makerspace. The items in this chapter could be perfect for your makerspace.

- Libraries may wish to lend tools for making as well as host making activities.
- Tinkering is a free-form activity that can inspire makers to greater creativity through experimenting with making tools.
- Minecraft is a popular creative game that can be a part of makerspace activities.

The next chapter examines stages in forming a makerspace.

◎ References

The Exploratory. 2015. "What Is Tinkering and Making." Learning Is Open. http://www.learningisopen.org/toolkit/tinkering-making.

Hultstrand, Aaron. 2015. "Minecraft in the Math Classroom: Methods, Benefits, and Difficulties of Minecraft Integration." Senior honors thesis, Liberty University. http://digitalcommons.liberty.edu/cgi/viewcontent.cgi?article=1591&context=honors.

Urban Libraries Council. 2016a. "Bricks and Beer." http://www.urbanlibraries.org/bricks---beer-innovation-1383.php?page_id=530.

———. 2016b. "International Seed Library Forum." http://www.urbanlibraries.org/international-seed-library-forum-innovation-1348.php?page_id=530.

———. 2016c. "Repair Cafe." http://www.urbanlibraries.org/repair-cafe-innovation-1379.php?page_id=530.

CHAPTER 11

Approaches for Developing a Makerspace That Enables Makers

NOW THAT YOU HAVE BUILT YOUR LIBRARY makerspace, how will you provide engaging programming for it? What will people do in it? How will it evolve? What will it become? So far we have discussed how to start a library makerspace as well as the variety of tools and technologies that can be used within. Next we consider how to manage the makerspace and how to sustain interest in it while continuing to meet the needs of your community.

⊙ Developing a Makerspace

A possible approach to this question is to visualize how you would form your makerspace from the beginning. Think of it as a chronological increase of activities and the ensuing permanence of the space and its services. Good (2013) suggests a set of stages that this development could follow, with the library making the leap from offering traditional library materials and activities to providing making activities. The stages as outlined do illustrate a fairly logical growth pattern for a makerspace. The textbox shows the stages suggested by Good.

Not every makerspace will follow the same process of development, by starting at the same place and then growing toward the ending phase. Makerspaces might start at stage 1 and work their way through to stage 5. Some may start at stage 3 and remain there, and there should be no prejudice shown toward a library that did not "evolve" to the end stage. Every makerspace should try to meet the needs and interests of its community, and that might not lead toward dirty labs or 3D printing.

A quick word on safety precautions is needed here. As new equipment comes into the makerspace, there needs to be training in using that equipment to be sure that a safe environment is maintained. Private makerspaces tend to require that makers take a class in using a laser cutter or a computer numerical control sewing machine before being able to use it independently. Librarians will need to think about how they will ensure that staff are trained in safe use of equipment and how patrons will be certified as having learned the proper techniques of operation, if they will be allowed to operate the equipment.

⊙ Makerspace Stages

Stage 1: One-off activities. Hold individual workshops or events showcasing a maker activity.

Stage 2: Ongoing meet-ups. Bring in an existing maker group on a regular basis and hold recurring programs.

Stage 3: Temporary tools and kits. Start to keep maker materials in the library and have them available for collaborative work in the library.

Stage 4: Clean labs. Create a dedicated space in the library that can accommodate some noise and some mild venting of fumes from laser cutters and 3D printers.

Stage 5: Dirty labs. Move to a space where louder and messier activities can happen, such as drilling, woodworking, and metalworking (Good, 2013).

⊙ Programming for Your Makerspace

Programming is a great way to garner and sustain awareness of your makerspace, and is a key facet of the makerspace experience. Whether it is an occasional workshop or demonstration event to interest people in the space or in the idea of making things or a more involved series of sessions, some thought needs to be given to how the programs will be offered and what options are available. The first question is who will be leading the sessions. In the informal survey of library makerspaces, respondents indicated who teaches training sessions, workshops, or classes in their makerspaces (respondents could choose more than one option). The most popular option was library staff members (chosen by 176 respondents, or 80 percent of all respondents), followed by volunteers (51 respondents, or 23 percent); other (50 respondents, or 23 percent), which may account for the fifty-five libraries still planning their makerspaces; and paid instructors from beyond the library (30 respondents, or 17 percent). It is clear from these results that a blend of instructors should be planned for but also that library staff will likely need to participate. This will have an impact on the training and professional development that must be provided to library staff. It may also mean that the talents and interests of library staff members may guide the library's initial choices of maker activities. Hopefully, volunteers and other experts can be located to enhance or expand those options, either from local makerspaces or from the library's larger community. There is information near the end of this chapter on finding makerspace mentors.

Next, you need to consider what sorts of programs will be offered. Since there are countless topics that could be addressed depending on the characteristics and audience of the makerspace, here are some general categories of sessions that could be created or pursued:

Demonstration session: an opportunity to show patrons how a particular making technology works or what could be created in the makerspace from a given activity. This session could be used to create general interest in the makerspace and to draw people into working on the equipment or activity that is highlighted.

Technology petting zoo: a display of technology items related to making that patrons could try out, with guidance, to gain familiarity with their options. This could be done

Figure 11.1. Word cloud of library makerspace survey responses on workshops and classes offered.

for a set period, or it could be left in place for a day or multiple days, provided that staff members would be available to assist patrons. This option is not unlike a demonstration session in its goals of marketing the makerspace, but it is less structured and very much a hands-on activity.

Instructional workshop: a dedicated session with a mixture of demonstration and hands-on activities to prepare patrons to make things. Generally, the goal would be for patrons to start working on a project that they could return to the makerspace and finish.

A series of workshops and/or demonstrations: could take a variety of forms, including a number of events on a single making technique that could build in level of difficulty or a calendar of independent events on different making activities, all presented in the course of a three-month period. The idea would be to have a regular set of programming in place. Patrons could choose to follow the whole series or jump into one area or level depending on their interests.

The teaching role of makerspaces is crucial to identifying and building a helping community that supports all makers. Some combination of these teaching methods will prime the pump for making to happen, and a sustained program of instruction will explore new areas for the development of the space and cause makers' skills to grow. Librarians have the tools and mind-set needed to make this happen, even if they may lack specific making skills. In the informal survey of library makerspaces, respondents were given the opportunity to share the types of workshops or classes that they offer. Figure 11.1 shows a word cloud of their responses, illustrating the variety of topics.

⊚ Programming for All Ages

The preceding chapters have not made a lot of distinctions about who the audience might be for a given making activity. While there are examples given throughout that represent activities and programs aimed at general age groups of participants, particularly school-age children in school and public library makerspaces, it is imperative to remember that makerspaces are for all patrons of all ages. In actuality, many other activities, from the simplest to the most complex, really could be undertaken by people of any age. The question here is to first consider whom you hope to reach with your makerspace and what impact you want it to have. Depending on the makeup of your library community, it might make sense to choose a particular demographic group to pilot the makerspace.

School libraries may have the easiest choice here, given that they primarily serve the students who take classes in the same building or on the same campus. Public libraries have the widest possible range of options on who might come to their programs, leading to a need either to aim programming at specific age ranges or to advertise events only to certain groups. Academic libraries will generally focus on students at their institutions but will likely reach out to faculty and staff members and may serve adults and others in their community. Once you identify your audience, you can sculpt programs to fit the individuals you hope to reach. You could, for instance, focus the makerspace and your programming on teens. As some libraries have found, that may lead to adults becoming interested in the makerspace, which can lead to an expansion of the makerspace or the creation of a whole new area for adults (if funding and space are available).

The situation to prepare for is one in which you are offering a makerspace with open hours for anyone to come in and use the materials and equipment. If it is truly open for anyone, you need to be ready for experienced makers to come in alongside families with toddlers. It is more a question of having age-appropriate activities and guidance available to meet the need. Hard age restrictions ("only available for patrons twelve and older") might make sense in some settings, such as using woodworking equipment or laser cutters, while ability may be the better deciding factor in others. That gets back to the idea of having required classes or training for using some equipment independently. Generally, you want to have an environment in which people have opportunities for making that fit their skill levels and interests. You may need to subdivide your programming to make that happen.

Transitioning Your Makerspace

Deciding whether and how to expand services is not a new concept for librarians, and makerspaces fit well into the framework. As interest grows in the makerspace, there will be calls to add types of making or to change the way the current items are made available. Looking back at the suggested stages at the beginning of this chapter, there are four key transitions that a library makerspace might want to make: open labs, dirty labs, noisy activities, dedicated spaces. All of these require a deeper commitment to the makerspace in that you are being called on to have library space used in particular ways for particular purposes. To make these transitions, you will need to take the makerspace seriously and show a greater intention to continue it as a service. Each of the four transitions is listed here, with a brief discussion on how it affects the library and the provision of the makerspace.

Open Lab

An open lab refers to having the makerspace or maker equipment available for patrons to use outside of specific class or workshop times. It might be a set time frame each day or just on certain days in the week. An open lab requires that library staff members or volunteers are available to assist people using the space, and it is predicated on there being enough interested makers to justify having that staffing available. Depending on the types of activities available, having an open lab might mean that the makerspace will need a dedicated space if it does not have one already. Or, any number of activities could be moved into a meeting room, a classroom within the library, or even an open seating area during the set times for open work. The important thing about having open work time in making is that it allows for unstructured work to happen and for makers to discover new things about the tools and processes they are using. Tinkering can truly happen in an open lab.

Dirty Lab

As noted at the start of this chapter, a dirty lab is a makerspace that accommodates messy activities such as woodworking or painting or cooking. Many maker activities can be pulled out and used in whatever space is available and then put away again. Lots of making can be messy, but the level of mess and relative ease of cleanup can keep making such as paper crafts, sewing, and 3D printing outside a dirty lab. With dirty lab activities, you are also likely to need dedicated space to keep equipment in place. Beyond just finding or creating a walled-off space, the furnishings, flooring, and facilities of the space should accommodate the making that is going to happen. If tables and chairs would be helpful to the making work, they should be able to stand up to the dirt created and be easily cleaned. Carpet must yield to more easily cleaned flooring. The requisite electrical outlets, lighting, and other added items should be installed, such as a sink to aid with cooking activities.

Noisy Activities

Noisy activities could describe various makerspace actions, from using any sort of cutting device to having a boisterous group of middle schoolers work with circuits. The primary thought here, though, is accommodating making that produces sound that is essential to the process but likely to distract others. This could just as easily describe audio-recording activities, such as the drum kit mentioned back in chapter 7, as well as the whine of drills and computer numerical control routers and the whirr of sewing machines. A space needs to have noise-cancellation or sound-dampening panels in place to work as a recording studio or a workroom.

Dedicated Spaces

A dedicated space, as noted in the other three transitions, is pretty much a requirement for a makerspace to take on the next level of activities or to have a chance to expand beyond occasional programming. Once again, as with the stages of development discussed earlier, there is no requirement that a library take on noisy or dirty activities or attempt to offer an open lab environment. Makerspaces can remain entirely mobile enterprises and move into action inside and beyond the library as programming needs dictate. But a permanent space, even one that is not perfectly outfitted for every possible use, gives the makerspace a sense of freedom and something of an anchored feeling. That space is helpful for holding programs that can be separate from the rest of the library and for storing items and equipment. Projects can be left unfinished in situ so that makers can return to them. Establishing a space for the makerspace is also a useful way to test out the limits of making possibilities within the library and to plan for either improving that space or building a new one.

Going Mobile

Makerspaces should not be limited to the narrow definition of making in a set-aside, dedicated space. Rather, think on a larger scale in that the making is happening somewhere in some space, even if that space is only temporarily focused on making. This is the concept behind the mobile makerspace experience, in which the making tools are brought to the space, used there, and then packed up and moved elsewhere for storage. The temporary space might be inside the library, outdoors, at a school, or anywhere in the community where you wish to bring it and someone agrees to having you make stuff. The mobile makerspace could involve a range of technologies, given that laptops and 3D printers are fairly mobile. It is an attempt to bring making to the people.

Thinking out the possibilities, the mobile makerspace might be the way that you start off with making activities in the library, bringing things out when needed into a shared common space and then returning them until the next program. The mobile makerspace might be a way to take some of the making activities from a dedicated space elsewhere, say, to a branch of a multilocation library system. Or it might be the only way that you offer making, as in the case of Maker Studio at the Springdale Public Library profiled in chapter 7, which didn't have room to expand and add a makerspace and instead simply rebranded their maker-type programming for teens and adults.

Kim Martin, Mary Compton, and Ryan Hunt teamed up to create Canada's first mobile makerspace out of a retrofitted 1989 school bus they named the MakerBus, which includes high-tech maker tools such as 3D printers and circuit kits as well as low-tech crafting supplies. As well, the Netherlands-based FryskLab is the first library-operated mobile makerspace in Europe and is a former library bus (Martin, Compton, and Hunt, 2017). This mobile concept can be more than just an introduction to making and is an option to pursue if it would fit your library.

Making Outside the Library

Going a step further, some libraries are even trying out the option of circulating maker-oriented items. On the one hand, this seems to work against some of the community-building and peer-guiding elements of a makerspace that work in a co-located space. On the other hand, circulating makerspace items follows a very traditional library model for getting things that people cannot buy into their hands to use. Someone who learns about a technology at a library makerspace event can then go home with that technology and make something.

Now, what are libraries circulating? The University of British Columbia Library lends Arduinos for a three-day loan. The North Carolina State University Hunt Library circulates 3D scanners and Makey Makeys. Many public and academic libraries are lending iPads and digital cameras and could add more maker-focused items.

There are a variety of electronics kits available that libraries could purchase and check out. One difficulty is that many of these kits are intended for a single project. This will likely get easier as more kits are produced with reuse in mind.

Incorporating Makerspace Mentors and Makers-in-Residence

As always, volunteers are a huge asset and can serve a variety of roles in the makerspace. These volunteers or mentors can teach classes, staff open times at the makerspace, or just assist patrons while working on their own projects. Mentors may come from a variety of backgrounds. They may be associated with a local makerspace, a hackerspace, or another making-related group, or they may just be individuals in the community with skills that they would like to share. As you plan your makerspace and talk with people in the community, you may meet individuals who could serve in a mentoring role. The *Makerspace Playbook* (Maker Media, 2013) has some guidance for creating a mentor interest survey. There may also be the opportunity to make a more formal arrangement with one or more mentors and establish a maker-in-residence program or to employ mentors to guide makerspace users (Ginsberg, 2017). This can bring a set of skills into the library that really adds to the community of your makerspace. The mentor or maker-in-residence could teach, demonstrate past and ongoing projects, and help patrons move toward making their own creations. The period of residence could be for a few workshops or for a longer period. STEAM Central at Stephens Central Library, profiled in chapter 8, received a grant for $75,000 to hire a maker-in-residence as well as make purchases for the makerspace.

Ⓖ Hosting Your Own Mini Maker Faire or Maker Camp

As Maker Faire events continue to gain popularity among the maker movement, consider hosting your own. According to Make Media, 215,000 people attended the two flagship Maker Faires in the Bay Area and New York in 2014 (Johnson, 2017). Also in 2014, the White House hosted its own Maker Faire. (Urban Libraries Council, 2017). Maker Faires offer chances for makers to show off their creations and their techniques. Maker Media sponsors some of the largest faires (http://makerfaire.com), the largest in the San Mateo/Bay Area, New York, and Chicago as well as a number of other cities and regions which have smaller events. These faires are great opportunities for libraries to market their makerspaces, to connect with other people who are interested in making, and to perhaps find interested mentors. In addition, the library could hold its own mini Maker Faire or maker day, in which the work of patron makers could be shown off and making activities demonstrated. Maker Media (2017a, 2017b) offers step-by-step guides to planning and organizing your own mini Maker Faires as well as how to run a school Maker Faire.

Another Maker Media–created opportunity is the annual Maker Camp (http://makezine.com/maker-camp), which is held each summer. The free event lasts for thirty days, and on each day, a new product is created. Videos on how to make the products are broadcast on Google Hangouts, and there are opportunities to interact with the maker camp counselors. Interested makers are provided with lists of materials so that they can plan ahead. It is a great source of making curriculum for you to use as you hold a summer

Figure 11.2. Intro to Arduino. *Image provided through a CC BY 2.0 License by SparkFunElectronics, http://www.flickr.com/photos/sparkfun/8167729010.*

making program (such as working with Arduinos, as shown in figure 11.2). You could structure a daily or weekly meeting to go over one or more projects and have this help kick off your own programming or supplement existing programming that you are doing.

You can also sign up to be an affiliate site for Maker Camp (at no charge), which will share your location through its website so that makers in your area can find you. The CreateSpace of the Middletown Public Library did this in 2013 and had an excellent experience with it.

ⓖ Listening to Your Makers and Guides

Amid all the making and deciding on programming and expanding space capabilities, it is imperative to look to two sources for information. They are the same sources that you used when gathering input on how to start the space, and they are just as important as the makerspace continues. First, be sure to talk to your makers and take the pulse of their making activities and their happiness with the space. You may follow some of the same routes you did when surveying potential makers or just touch base with individuals on occasion. You want to make sure that their needs are being met and that the space continues to interest them. It is also very important to watch and see if new people are coming to your programming and dropping into the space. You want to make sure that the makerspace is not becoming a closed circle but one that is growing and taking in new people and new challenges.

Second, keep listening to the wisdom of those who have preceded you in creating library makerspaces or those who are newly coming alongside you. That advice was helpful as you created your own plan and story for what a library makerspace could be. Now you can use those articles, websites, or conversations to keep on track and continue to succeed. Stay aware of new trends in technology and new applications in makerspace environments. The resources in chapter 12 will help you stay on track. Be sure to not just watch for new stuff but actually try new things out. And the knowledge from the maker movement and library maker community should lead you back to your patrons to see what they think of these possibilities.

ⓖ Key Points

Library makerspaces offer many programming and service possibilities.

There are several stages or transitions that library makerspaces can go through.

- Workshops, trainings, and classes can be taught by library staff, volunteers, or paid instructors from beyond the library. There are several types of training sessions to choose from.
- Makerspaces can be mobile, and making can happen at home with circulating maker technologies.
- Identifying maker mentors and establishing makers-in-residence programs can add guidance, coordination, and enthusiasm to your makerspace programs.
- Maker Faires, mini Maker Faires, and Maker Camp are great opportunities to inspire library staff and patrons and to teach skills.

The book concludes with a chapter on keeping track of makerspace happenings and considering how the library can alter its role to include makerspaces.

⊚ References

Ginsberg, Sharona. 2017. "Sustainability: Keeping the Library Makerspace Alive." In *The Makerspace Librarian's Sourcebook*, edited by Ellyssa Kroski, 325–344. Chicago: American Library Association.

Good, Travis. 2013. "Making Makerspace Libraries." YouTube, March 28. http://www.youtube.com/watch?v=WV_Eu5Kz1cA&feature=youtu.be.

Johnson, Eric. 2017. "The Future of Library Makerspaces." In *The Makerspace Librarian's Sourcebook*, edited by Ellyssa Kroski, 345–367. Chicago: American Library Association.

Maker Media. 2013. *Makerspace Playbook, School Edition.* http://makerspace.com/wp-content/uploads/2013/02/MakerspacePlaybook-Feb2013.pdf.

———. 2017a. "How to Make a Maker Faire." Maker Faire. http://makerfaire.com/global.

———. 2017b. "How to Make a School Maker Faire." Maker Faire. http://makerfaire.com/global/school.

Martin, Kim, Mary Compton, and Ryan Hunt. 2017. "Mobile Makerspaces." In *The Makerspace Librarian's Sourcebook*, edited by Ellyssa Kroski, 307–323. Chicago: American Library Association.

Urban Libraries Council. 2017. "Makerspaces in Libraries." http://www.urbanlibraries.org/-makerspaces-in-libraries-pages-338.php.

CHAPTER 12

Remaking the Library?

Tracking the Present and Future of Making in Libraries

IN THIS CHAPTER

▷ Framing the Future of Makerspaces

▷ Sharing Patron Creations and Making Their Own

▷ Staying Current on Making

▷ Completing the First Leg of the Journey

AS LIBRARY MAKERSPACES CONTINUE to grow and evolve, librarians must endeavor to keep abreast of new developments, including new tools and techniques for making as well as trends in the field. There is a wealth of information and resources available that provide news and advice about the larger maker domain as well as a plethora of library-specific makerspace news outlets. The future of library makerspaces will largely depend on how well librarians keep in touch with their community needs, learn from the experiences of those who have already built successful library makerspaces, and keep aware of new trends and technologies in this steadily developing field. This chapter will explore the many tools and resources for keeping current as well as channels and sources to keep in touch with fellow library makers.

Framing the Future of Makerspaces

Library makerspaces have been growing at an increasing rate. While there are still many libraries and communities that do not yet have makerspaces, they are quickly becoming a familiar sight in libraries today. As a matter of fact, the Urban Libraries Council (2017) has a list of over forty library makerspaces in the United States alone. According to Miguel Figueroa, director of the Center for the Future of Libraries at the American Library Association, "Makerspaces are part of libraries' expanded mission to be places where people can not only consume knowledge, but create new knowledge" (Fallows, 2016).

And as more of these new spaces appear, it will be interesting to watch how they develop. Every new makerspace is the result of a combination of local needs and influences from the wider network of makers. They are not exact copies of earlier models, and even if they start in a mode driven by work elsewhere, they cannot remain static. Each makerspace has the potential to do something transformative with making activities and then influence that wider network. You can expect that the makerspaces of today will continue to evolve as their numbers swell. New technologies will come, and older ways of making will continue to be rediscovered and perhaps refined or altered by technology and new approaches.

One meaningful impact will not be exclusively technological but rather social. Although makerspaces are available in many libraries for people of all ages, there is a significant focus on providing learning opportunities for children. As school library makerspaces grow, the opportunities for students to participate in making activities will grow beyond the options that they might have in art, science, and shop classes. If children are increasingly working on STEM and STEAM projects in the library and in classrooms, they will join a larger audience of people who might be interested in making things on an ongoing basis. Makerspaces are steadily becoming recognized as important tools in education (Costello, Powers, and Haugh, 2017). Will growing numbers of kids who have experienced making be more likely to pursue makerspace experiences at their schools, in their public libraries, and on college campuses? That might happen.

When you look to the future, it is often hard to see beyond the next week or the next fiscal year. Given the immediacy of this view and the expectations that it allows, it is still possible to see if a broader sense of the future can be deduced from expressed needs. In chapter 4, there is a section on what is missing from the makerspaces in the informal survey of makerspaces in libraries. In that section, respondents suggested twelve categories of things that they would like to add to their makerspaces in the coming year. Table 12.1 lists those categories (in order of popularity).

There is a nice blend in these categories of high technology along with lower-level but high-skill technologies. You can also see a representation of the space in which to use these tools and technologies as well as instruction and the staff to provide it. What ties this all together is the evolution of the types of tools that makerspaces are including in their creation spaces and the hope for additional events that bring people together to learn about making and demonstrate what they have made. If this says anything about the future of makerspaces in libraries, it is perhaps that the libraries of the moment are focused on expanding their making options, finding more room to make things, and teaching more people how to make. If that is what can be expected from library makerspaces in the future, then this experiment will become all the more substantial in presence and reach.

One huge expected development with making tools is that they could eventually enable a makerspace or a home user to create and repair many objects and products without turning to manufacturers or retailers. This empowers consumers to create their own parts for existing products as well as invent brand new ones.

Table 12.1. Top Twelve Wish List Items for Next Year

WISH LIST ITEMS	N
3D printer/3D modeling/3D scanner	40
Sewing machines and fabric arts	21
Virtual reality equipment	12
More space	11
Robotics	10
Legos	10
Laser cutter	10
Workshops and classes	9
CNC machines	7
Video and audio production equipment	6
Coding	6
More staff	4

This is not to say that everyone will have a positive response to these developments or even understand what a makerspace is or why the library has it. Library makers must expect that makerspaces will be questioned in their communities and will not have an easy road to universal acceptance. Chapter 2 discusses some reasons for having a makerspace at all, particularly in the library.

Sharing Patron Creations and Making Their Own

Libraries are better positioned than other entities to host a makerspace for two main reasons: first, they can serve as a mechanism to share the created items on behalf of patrons; second, makerspaces can create stuff that improves library services. On the first point, libraries are well suited to being physical and virtual repositories for stuff. Does the library become a place for its makers to display what they have made or to share the open-source creations that they wish to offer the world? There is a great analogy related to making—namely, whether the library should be a grocery store, where people get the information bits they need, or a kitchen, where people put the information together in a final product (Valenza, 2008). Is there a way for a library to also be a dining room or a restaurant, where people beyond the library and other than the maker come to use and maybe even buy the end product?

On the second point, there are at least two good reasons for library staff members to get into making beyond their role of supporting a makerspace for others. Modeling creation will help staff understand the activities and technologies involved and can provide an example for their patrons and the larger community of makers. Focusing their creative efforts on library-related problems or needs can help them improve or expand their services in some way. There are some interesting examples in the projects list and blog at http://www.librarytestkitchen.org, and this is only the beginning of possibilities.

As libraries begin to host makerspaces, the interplay of maker culture and library culture should lead to some intriguing developments.

Staying Current on Making

With the continued rise of the makerspaces-in-libraries movement, it will be increasingly imperative to be aware of larger trends and to follow up on specific technologies and project ideas. Fortunately, there are many websites, electronic discussion groups, and other resources available for making, makerspaces in general, and library makerspaces. The following list of resources, while far from complete, was compiled through investigations and the suggestions of respondents to the informal survey of makerspaces in libraries (see the appendix for details).

General Resources

Make: (http://makezine.com): The website for *Make:* magazine contains a blog, videos, project information, and links to the other Maker Media sites. The projects are sorted by category and rated for difficulty.

Maker book lists (http://jocolibrary.bibliocommons.com/lists/show/98731951_jclmeredithn): This page provides a series of maker book lists created by Meredith Nelson, Johnson County Public Library, organized by age and by type of making. It is a great place to track down some maker titles for your library collection.

Maker Education Initiative (http://www.makered.org): Sponsored by Maker Media, Intel, Cognizant, and Pixar, the Maker Education Initiative is dedicated to getting kids making. The site provides free resources to help plan programs.

Maker Faire (http://makerfaire.com): This site advertises Maker Faires and provides information on taking part in them. It is a very helpful way to find a maker event near you.

The Maker Mom (http://www.themakermom.com): This blog highlights making resources and is especially focused on STEM resources for kids.

Tech Age Kids (http://www.techagekids.com): This website has hundreds of project ideas for everything from coding to Raspberry Pi to robots and electronics, geared specifically for children.

YOUmedia Network (http://www.youmedia.org): YOUmedia manages digital learning labs for youth in a variety of locations. It offers a toolkit for forming a makerspace program and links to resources that can help in the planning process.

Directories

Makerspace.com has a directory of makerspaces at https://spaces.makerspace.com/directory/, and the *Make:* magazine site has a list of maker community groups at http://makerfaire.com/maker-community-groups. The MakerMap (http://themakermap.com) is an open-source directory of making organizations and sites that provides a searchable

Google Maps interface to help you locate local and regional makers. Similar sources include Hackerspaces (http://hackerspaces.org/wiki/List_of_Hackerspaces) and MIT's Fab Lab List (http://www.fabfoundation.org/index.php/fab-labs/).

Library-Specific Resources

Build-a-Lab Digital Media Lab Training Series (http://heritage.utah.gov/library/build-a-lab): This site hosts a series of four archived webinars sponsored by the Utah State Library in 2014 on digital media labs and makerspaces around the United States. Provides information on how the labs were created and the services they offer.

Library as Incubator Project (http://www.libraryasincubatorproject.org): This blog highlights the connections between artists and libraries and shares creative opportunities and resources.

Library Makers (http://librarymakers.blogspot.com): This blog is dedicated to promoting making projects, particularly ones aimed toward children and focused on arts and crafts.

Library MakerSpaces (http://www.pinterest.com/cari_young/library-makerspaces): This is a Pinterest board with links to many maker projects and products. It is a great way to browse for projects.

Make It at the Library—Makerspace Resources (http://libraries.idaho.gov/make-it-at-the-library): This site, created by the Idaho Commission for Libraries, provides a collection of makerspace examples, funding resources, and making materials.

MakerBridge (http://makerbridge.si.umich.edu): This site offers discussion forums for people working in library makerspaces, as well as a blog and lists of recommended tools for making.

Makerspaces (http://youthserviceslibrarianship.wikispaces.com/Makerspaces): This is an excellent collection of makerspace resources created by students in the University of Illinois Graduate School of Library and Information Science as part of a larger wiki entitled "Youth Services Librarianship: A Guide to Working with Young People in School and Public Libraries."

Multimedia Project Guide (http://libraryguides.oswego.edu/toolbox): This guide is filled with resources on presentations, multimedia production, and 3D printing, developed by Emily Thompson at SUNY Oswego.

Books

Hundreds of quality maker-related books can be found through the Maker Media books and magazines catalog at https://www.makershed.com/collections/books-magazines. You might also start with some of these:

Carey, Anne. 2016. *STEAM Kids: 50+ Science/Technology/Engineering/Art/Math Hands-On Projects for Kids*. CreateSpace Independent Publishing.

Challoner, Jack. 2016. *Maker Lab: 28 Super Cool Projects: Build * Invent * Create * Discover*. New York: DK Children.

Graves, Colleen, and Aaron Graves. 2016. *The Big Book of Makerspace Projects: Inspiring Makers to Experiment, Create, and Learn.* New York: McGraw-Hill Education TAB.

Kroski, Ellyssa. 2017. *63 Ready-to-Use Maker Projects.* Chicago: American Library Association.

Kroski, Ellyssa. 2017. *The Makerspace Librarian's Sourcebook.* Chicago: American Library Association.

Martinez, Sylvia Libow. 2013. *Invent to Learn: Making, Tinkering, and Engineering in the Classroom.* Torrance, CA: Constructing Modern Knowledge Press.

Wilkinson, Karen, and Mike Petrich. 2014. *The Art of Tinkering.* San Francisco: Weldon Owen.

Project Sites

Adafruit Learning System (http://learn.adafruit.com): This site is a collection of tutorials and project ideas for working with Arduino, Raspberry Pi, LilyPad, circuits, 3D printing, and more.

Cubeecraft (http://www.cubeecraft.com): This site has a collection of paper craft patterns of various types that can be printed for folding.

Instructables.com (http://www.instructables.com): Instructables is the place to find project instructions to make all sorts of things. If something can be made, there is probably a video here on how to make it. You can also post your own projects here.

Make It at Your Library (http://makeitatyourlibrary.org): A cooperative project of ILEAD USA graduates (a library leadership program) and Instructables.com, the site offers various types of making projects. The projects can be sorted by topic, age level, time to complete, and cost.

Pinterest (https://www.pinterest.com): A search of this inspiration-filled website will bring back thousands of pins about makerspace ideas, crafts, DIY projects, and so on.

Thingiverse (http://thingiverse.com): This site is a repository of 3D designs that are open for anyone to modify or print using a 3D printer. You can find additional 3D design collections in chapter 9.

Products

Afinia (http://www.afinia.com): This site offers information on using your Afinia 3D printer and a gallery of printed projects.

Arduino (http://arduino.cc): The Arduino site offers project information and support for using Arduinos.

Chibitronics (https://chibitronics.com): This is the vendor site for circuit sticker kits, copper tape, LED light stickers, sensor stickers, and classroom packs for instructors.

Digi-key Electronics (https://www.digikey.com): This is the vendor site for affordable electronics and coin cell batteries for projects.

I Am Cardboard (http://www.imcardboard.com): This is the vendor site for affordable Google Cardboard and other virtual reality headsets.

MakerBot (http://makerbot.com): This is a 3D printer's vendor site and offers many bits of advice on 3D printing along with information on its products.

Maker Shed (http://makershed.com): Maker Shed is the official store of *Make:* magazine.

Makey Makey (http://www.makeymakey.com): This is the vendor site for Makey Makey classic, Makcy Makey Go, Classroom Invention Literacy Kit, and so on.

Materials, Tools, and Kits (http://libraries.idaho.gov/page/materials-tools-and-kits): This website has a lengthy list of maker products with links to purchase them or learn more about them.

Raspberry Pi (http://raspberrypi.org): This site provides projects and support to use with Raspberry Pi.

SparkFun Electronics (http://www.sparkfun.com): This site is a great place to shop for electronic gadgets, including items for e-textiles, robotics, circuits, and Raspberry Pis. The company offers educator kits, which are bulk amounts of materials to get a whole class making.

Funding and Donation Sources

DonorsChoose (http://www.donorschoose.org): Public school teachers can post their classroom needs on this site and then see if donors will choose to fund them. It could be a resource for your school library makerspace to seek some equipment.

GoFundMe (https://www.gofundme.com): This is a fund-raising website for charities that is used by many libraries to raise money.

Institute of Museum and Library Services—Learning Labs in Libraries and Museums (http://www.imls.gov/about/learning_labs.aspx): This site highlights a series of grant programs offered to help create digital learning labs in libraries and museums, with links to successfully funded programs and resources related to digital literacy and projects.

TechSoup (http://www.techsoup.org): TechSoup is an organization that collects donated technology from partner organizations and distributes it to nonprofit organizations and libraries.

Discussion Lists

Create (http://www.cvl-lists.org/mailman/listinfo/create): This list is designed for those working with library makerspaces.

K–12 Digital Fabrication Labs (bit.ly/k12fablabgroup): This Google Group is primarily aimed at K–12 makerspaces and maker activities.

Librarymakerspace-1 (https://lists.ufl.edu/cgi-bin/wa?A0=LIBRARYMAKER-SPACE-L): This discussion list is for librarians with library makerspaces.

LITA Maker Technology Interest Group (http://lists.ala.org/sympa/info/lita-makertech): This group discusses technologies located within makerspaces, content creation spaces, and the management of such areas.

Tweeting and Following

The following list shows Twitter (http://twitter.com) hashtags, search terms, and Twitter accounts to follow for information on making. There are many more out there, depending on your specific making interests, but these will get you started:

#3Dprinting

#librarymakerspace

#maker

#makers

#makerspace (with or without "library")

#STEMchat ("makerspace")

@make

@makerbridge

@makered

@makezine

Facebook Groups

There are two groups with a specific focus on library makerspaces. You can find similarly minded individuals here to share your makerspace questions:

Library Entrepreneurship and Maker Services, https://www.facebook.com/groups/startup.library

Makerspaces and the Participatory Library, https://www.facebook.com/groups/librarymaker

Technology Sites and Blogs

ALA TechSource (http://www.alatechsource.org/blog): The American Library Association's TechSource blog provides discussions on many technologies used in libraries and elsewhere; it has covered makerspace developments in libraries.

Boing Boing (http://boingboing.net): This blog features all sorts of interesting stories about technology and culture. It covers topics that might be of interest to makers, including ones that directly mention makers and makerspaces.

EDUCAUSE (http://educause.edu): This site and blog focus on developments in technology that affect higher education.

Engadget (http://engadget.com): This site and blog cover news on and reviews of many technology products.

Gizmodo (http://gizmodo.com): This site and blog feature stories about technology news and products.

Mashable (http://mashable.com): This site and blog cover news and resources related to our digital world.

The Next Web (http://thenextweb.com): This blog focuses on international technology news.

ReadWrite (http://readwrite.com): *ReadWrite* is a technology news blog.

Wired (http://www.wired.com): The blog for *Wired* magazine reports on many technology issues including online resources.

◉ Completing the First Leg of the Journey

In this book, you have seen the rise of makers and the inclusion of maker activities in the work of libraries. As this is still a new service and a new reason for libraries to provide equipment, space, and programming, time will tell if makerspaces will last in libraries, be better placed in larger communities of makers, or fade altogether. What seems certain is that as long as people are curious about how things work, they will take them apart and try to make them work again, work better, or work differently. As this process continues, people will gain skills that they can pass on to others. Making will not end, nor will the teaching and sharing of making knowledge. As libraries continue in their mission as community-gathering spaces dedicated to the sharing of knowledge, it seems well in keeping with this mission to provide the means to make, the space to gather in, and the access to the knowledge that keeps making happening. Libraries should investigate making and see what they can provide to help their communities.

◉ Key Points

- The future of library makerspaces appears bright if they pursue equipment, space, and community-building events as needed parts of makerspaces.
- Libraries should seek ways to apply their traditional skills to serve makers and develop new library products by accepting the challenge of applying making.
- There are many resources to turn to for more information on many aspects of library makerspaces.

◉ References

Costello, Laura, Meredith Powers, and Dana Haugh. 2017. "Pedagogy and Prototyping in Library Makerspaces." In *The Makerspace Librarian's Sourcebook*, edited by Ellyssa Kroski, 29–36. Chicago: American Library Association.

Fallows, Deborah. 2016. "How Libraries Are Becoming Modern Makerspaces." *Atlantic*, March 11. https://www.theatlantic.com/technology/archive/2016/03/everyone-is-a-maker/473286/.

Urban Libraries Council. 2017. "Makerspaces in Libraries." http://www.urbanlibraries.org/-makerspaces-in-libraries-pages-338.php.

Valenza, Joyce. 2008. "Library as Domestic Metaphor." *Neverending Search* (blog), August 25. http://blogs.slj.com/neverendingsearch/2008/08/25/library-as-domestic-metaphor/.

Appendix: Makerspaces in Libraries Survey

⑥ Overview

During April 2017, I (Ellyssa) conducted a web-based survey on makerspaces in libraries. It was created using SurveyMonkey. Librarians were asked to respond anonymously. The survey was distributed through two Facebook groups (Makerspaces and the Participatory Library and Library Entrepreneurship and Maker Services), and the following list of library electronic discussion groups:

- ARLIS-L@lsv.arlisna.org, Art Libraries Society of North America
- cjc-l@ala.org, ACRL Community and Junior Colleges section
- code4lib@listserv.nd.edu, Coders for Libraries discussion
- COLLIB-L@ala.org, ACRL College Libraries section
- create@cvl-lists.org, discussion of creation and makerspaces in libraries
- lis-pub-libs@jiscmail.ac.uk, UK Public Libraries
- lita-l@ala.org, Library and Information Technology Association
- lm_net@listserv.syr.edu, School Library Media and Network Communications
- publib@webjunction.org, OCLC Public Librarianship
- sla-dite@sla.lyris.net, Special Libraries Association—IT Division
- uls-l@ala.org, ACRL University Libraries Section
- alsc-l@lists.ala.org, ALSC-L Association for Library Service to Children List

There were 273 respondents. In response to the question "Does your library provide a makerspace or a similar space?" 164 (60 percent) of the respondents answered yes, 55 (20 percent) are planning to start makerspaces in the near future, and 54 (20 percent) are not currently providing makerspaces nor are planning to do so. The following responses all come from the 219 librarians who currently provide makerspaces or who plan to soon start a makerspace. Their responses to each of the fifteen questions are summarized as follows.

"What Type of Library Do You Work In?"

Table A.1. "What Type of Library Do You Work In?"

	RESPONDENTS	
	%	N
Public	42.9	94
Academic	33.8	74
School	22.4	49
Special	0.9	2
Other	0.0	0

"Where Is Your Library Located (State/Province/Country)?"

Librarians from forty-four US states responded to the survey along with librarians from five other countries: Australia (eight), United Kingdom (eight), Canada (four), Egypt (one), and Ireland (one).

Table A.2. "Where Is Your Library Located?"

STATE	RESPONDENTS, N	STATE	RESPONDENTS, N
Alabama	2	Nebraska	3
Arizona	4	Nevada	1
Arkansas	1	New Hampshire	3
California	7	New Jersey	7
Colorado	7	New Mexico	1
Connecticut	4	New York	9
Delaware	1	North Carolina	6
Florida	7	North Dakota	1
Georgia	10	Ohio	4
Idaho	14	Oklahoma	2
Illinois	8	Oregon	7
Indiana	1	Pennsylvania	3
Iowa	4	Rhode Island	2
Kansas	2	South Carolina	1
Kentucky	2	Tennessee	7
Louisiana	1	Texas	19

STATE	RESPONDENTS, _N_	STATE	RESPONDENTS, _N_
Maine	1	Virginia	6
Maryland	14	Washington	3
Massachusetts	3	Washington, DC	1
Minnesota	4	Wisconsin	4
Mississippi	1	Wyoming	2
Missouri	4		

"What Do You Call Your Makerspace?"

A selection of these comments is included in chapter 3.

"How Long Has Your Space Been in Place?"

Table A.3. "How Long Has Your Space Been in Place?"

	RESPONDENTS	
	%	N
1–2 years	26.9	59
<1 year	26.0	57
Not yet started	18.3	40
2–3 years	15.5	34
3–4 years	7.3	16
>4 years	5.9	13

"Did the Funding to Start Your Makerspace Come From . . . ?"

Funding for the makerspaces came from a variety of sources. Respondents chose one or more of the following ways that their makerspaces could be funded. Respondents were able to select more than one response, so the total percentage will be higher than 100 percent.

Table A.4. "Did the Funding to Start Your Makerspace Come From . . . ?"

	RESPONDENTS	
	%	N
The library budget	53.9	118
Grants	40.6	89
Donations	35.6	78
Additional funding from your parent organization	16.0	35
Other	8.2	18

Respondents were asked to share specifics about grants and donation sources; table A.5 shows the most popular results, and table A.6 shows the rest.

Table A.5. Top Fifteen Donation Sources

DONATION SOURCES	NN
Friends of the Library	11
Patron donations	11
Self-funded	8
Local/district education foundation	7
PTA	6
LSTA Grant	6
IMLS Grant	6
DonorsChoose.org	4
Idaho STEM Action Center	3
Staff donations	3
The Library Foundation	2
YEI Project	2
European Social Fund	2
State grant program	2
National Library of Medicine Grant	2

Table A.6. Other Sources of Grants and Donations

Other Sources
Alabama Digital Humanities Grant
Allstate Foundation
ALSC Curiosity Creates Grant
Ann Sherry Foundation
Arts Council Grant
The Associated Colleges of the Midwest Faculty Career Enhancement Grant
Best Buy Community Grant
Boise Education Foundation Grant
CCC Makerspace Grant
Central Texas Library System Grant
Clay Electric Round-Up grant program
Community Foundation for Palm Beach and Martin Counties

Community Trust Foundation Grant

Connecticut State Library Grant

Durham Foundation Grant

General Electric

Green Bay Packers Community Foundation

Hancher Foundation

The InfyMakers Grant

Knights Foundation

Kohler Foundation

Laura H Moore Cunningham Foundation

Local community grants

Local councilors community grants fund

Local humanitarian fair

Local thrift stores

Lowe's Educators Grant

Lowe's stores

McElroy Trust

Mead Public Library Foundation

Mott Foundation

The National Writing Project Grant

OCLC

Pacific Library Partnership Innovation Grant

Perloff Family Foundation (local to Maine)

Protect Next Generation State of Illinois

PTO Grant

Reading Olympics

Scholastic Dollars

State Farm

State Library Partnership

Stewarts Shops

Student donations

Thomas Family Grant

TSLAC

21st Century Grant

The Weller Foundation

"Do You Charge for Any of the Following Items in Your Makerspace?"

Ninety-nine respondents (45 percent of all respondents) reported that their makerspaces charge (or will be charging) for items. Respondents were able to select more than one response, so the total percentage will be higher than 100 percent. The "other" category represents makerspaces that do not charge or are undecided about charging at this time.

Table A.7. "Do You Charge for Any of the Following Items in Your Makerspace?"

	RESPONDENTS	
	%	N
Other (please specify)	61.6	135
Supplies used in making	34.7	76
Fees for classes or workshops	4.1	9
Equipment use	3.7	8
Membership fee	2.7	6

"When People Ask You Why You Have a Makerspace, What Do You Tell Them?"

A selection of these comments is included in chapter 2.

"What Kinds of Tools or Equipment or Creation Options Does Your Makerspace Have?"

Respondents were able to select more than one response, so the total percentage will be higher than 100 percent.

Table A.8. "What Kinds of Tools or Equipment or Creation Options Does Your Makerspace Have?"

	RESPONDENTS	
TECHNOLOGY/ACTIVITY	%	N
Computer workstations	66.7	146
3D printing	65.8	144
Arts and crafts	64.8	142
Computer programming/software	48.4	106
3D modeling	46.6	102
Photo editing	45.2	99
Video editing	43.4	95
Tinkering	43.4	95
Arduino/Raspberry Pi	41.6	91

TECHNOLOGY/ACTIVITY	RESPONDENTS	
	%	N
Robotics	36.5	80
Scanning photos to digital	33.8	74
Other (please specify)	33.3	73
Electronics	30.1	66
Fabric shop (sewing machines, leather sewing machines, CNC embroidery machines, etc.)	28.8	63
Vinyl cutting	25.6	56
Soldering iron	24.7	54
Animation	23.3	51
Digital music recording	22.8	50
Creating a website or online portfolio	22.4	49
High-quality scanner	22.4	49
Prototyping	19.6	43
Soft circuits	19.6	43
Game creation	18.3	40
Inventing	16.9	37
Circuit hacking	16.0	35
VHS conversion equipment	13.7	30
Electronic music programming	12.3	27
Laser cutting	11.9	26
Electronic book production	9.6	21
Digital scrapbooking	9.1	20
Large format printer	9.1	20
Computer numerical control (CNC) machines	9.1	20
Creating apps	8.2	18
Woodworking (table saw, panel saw, bandsaw, drill press, etc.)	5.9	13
Food/culinary arts	5.5	12
Mobile development	4.6	10
Jewelry making (acetylene torch, buffing station, annealing pans, forming tools, etc.)	4.6	10
Plastics/composites	4.6	10
Milling machine	4.1	9
Screen printing	3.7	8
Industrial sewing machine	3.7	8
Silk screening	1.8	4

(Continued)

Table A.8. *(Continued)*

TECHNOLOGY/ACTIVITY	RESPONDENTS	
	%	N
Bicycle building/maintenance	1.4	3
Ceramics	1.4	3
Mold making	0.9	2
Potter's wheel and kiln	0.9	2
Letterpress	0.9	2
Stained glass	0.9	2
Welding	0.9	2
Dark room	0.5	1
Blacksmithing	0.5	1
Metal shop (metal lathe, cold saw, horizontal bandsaw, sheet metal, etc.)	0.5	1
Automotive	0.0	0
Guitar repair	0.0	0
Glass shop (glass blowing, kiln, jewelry making, etc.)	0.0	0

"How Did You Decide What Technologies to Offer in Your Makerspace?"

Respondents were able to select more than one response, so the total percentage will be higher than 100 percent.

Table A.9. "How Did You Decide What Technologies to Offer in Your Makerspace?"

	RESPONDENTS	
	%	N
Modeled on other makerspaces	61.2	134
Suggestions from patrons	42.9	94
Input from educators	40.6	89
Other	32.4	71
Donations of equipment	26.9	59
Patron surveys	13.7	30

"What Items or Technologies Get the Most Use in Your Makerspace?"

A selection of these comments is included in chapter 4.

"What Kinds of Classes, Workshops, or Training Do You Provide in or for Your Makerspace?"

A selection of these comments is included in chapter 11.

"Are Trainings, Workshops, or Classes Taught By . . . ?"

Respondents were able to select more than one response, so the total percentage will be higher than 100 percent.

Table A.10. "Are Trainings, Workshops, or Classes Taught by . . . ?"

	RESPONDENTS	
	%	N
Library staff	80.4	176
Volunteers	23.3	51
Other	22.8	50
Paid instructors from beyond the library	16.9	37

"What Are Your Go-To Resources to Stay Aware of Developments That Could Impact Your Makerspace?"

A selection of these resources is included in chapter 12.

"What Do You Hope to Add to Your Makerspace in the Next Year?"

A selection of these comments is included in chapter 4.

Bibliography

All That 3D. 2017. "10 Insane Benefits of 3D Printing." https://www.allthat3d.com/3d-printing-benefits.

ATX Hackerspace. 2017. "Laser Cutter Materials." http://atxhs.org/wiki/Laser_Cutter_Materials.

Bronkar, Cherie. 2017. "How to Start a Library Makerspace." In *The Makerspace Librarian's Sourcebook*, edited by Ellyssa Kroski, 3–28. Chicago: American Library Association.

Clark, Chad. 2017. "Library Hackerspace Programs." In *The Makerspace Librarian's Sourcebook*, edited by Ellyssa Kroski, 287–303. Chicago: American Library Association.

Colegrove, Tod. 2017. "Editorial Board Thoughts: Arts into Science, Technology, Engineering, and Mathematics—STEAM, Creative Abrasion, and the Opportunity in Libraries Today." *Information Technology and Libraries* 36 (1): 4–10.

Costello, Laura, Meredith Powers, and Dana Haugh. 2017. "Pedagogy and Prototyping in Library Makerspaces." In *The Makerspace Librarian's Sourcebook*, edited by Ellyssa Kroski, 29–36. Chicago: American Library Association.

Daring Librarian. 2015. "Makerspace Starter Kit." June 6. http://www.thedaringlibrarian.com/2015/06/makerspace-starter-kit.html.

Delecki, Kevin. 2017. "Safety and Guidelines in the Library Makerspace." In *The Makerspace Librarian's Sourcebook*, edited by Ellyssa Kroski, 73–84. Chicago: American Library Association.

Dumas, Rob. 2017. "Computer Numerical Control in the Library with Cutting and Milling Machines." In *The Makerspace Librarian's Sourcebook*, edited by Ellyssa Kroski, 229–244. Chicago: American Library Association.

Egbert, Megan. 2017. "Lilypad, Adafruit, and More: Wearable Electronics for Libraries." In *The Makerspace Librarian's Sourcebook*, edited by Ellyssa Kroski, 157–173. Chicago: American Library Association.

The Exploratory. 2015. "What Is Tinkering and Making?" Learning Is Open. http://www.learningisopen.org/toolkit/tinkering-making.

Fallows, Deborah. 2016. "How Libraries Are Becoming Modern Makerspaces." *Atlantic*, March 11. https://www.theatlantic.com/technology/archive/2016/03/everyone-is-a-maker/473286/.

Ginsberg, Sharona. 2017. "Sustainability: Keeping the Library Makerspace Alive." In *The Makerspace Librarian's Sourcebook*, edited by Ellyssa Kroski, 325–344. Chicago: American Library Association.

Good, Travis. 2013. "Making Makerspace Libraries." YouTube, March 28. http://www.youtube.com/watch?v=WV_Eu5Kz1cA&feature=youtu.be.

Harrop, Wendy. 2017. "littleBits, Makey Makey, Chibitronics, and More: Circuitry Projects for Libraries." In *The Makerspace Librarian's Sourcebook*, edited by Ellyssa Kroski, 213–228. Chicago: American Library Association.

"A History of Making." 2013. *American Libraries* 44 (1/2): 46.

Hoffman, Tony. 2017. "The Best 3D Printers of 2017." *PC Magazine*, January 18. http://www.pcmag.com/article2/0,2817,2470038,00.asp.

Hultstrand, Aaron. 2015. "Minecraft in the Math Classroom: Methods, Benefits, and Difficulties of Minecraft Integration." Senior honors thesis, Liberty University. http://digitalcommons.liberty.edu/cgi/viewcontent.cgi?article=1591&context=honors.

Johnson, Eric. 2017. "The Future of Library Makerspaces." In *The Makerspace Librarian's Sourcebook*, edited by Ellyssa Kroski, 345–367. Chicago: American Library Association.

Kim, Bohyun. 2017. "A Librarian's Guide to 3D Printing." In *The Makerspace Librarian's Sourcebook*, edited by Ellyssa Kroski, 87–112. Chicago: American Library Association.

Kroski, Ellyssa. 2017. *The Makerspace Librarian's Sourcebook*. Chicago: American Library Association.

Maker Ed. 2015. *Youth Makerspace Playbook*. Maker Education Initiative. http://makered.org/wp-content/uploads/2015/09/Youth-Makerspace-Playbook_FINAL.pdf.

Maker Faire. 2017. "Meet the Makers." http://makerfaire.com/bay-area-2017/meet-the-makers/.

Maker Media. 2013. *Makerspace Playbook, School Edition*. http://makerspace.com/wp-content/uploads/2013/02/MakerspacePlaybook-Feb2013.pdf.

———. 2017a. "How to Make a Maker Faire." Maker Faire. http://makerfaire.com/global.

———. 2017b. "How to Make a School Maker Faire." Maker Faire. http://makerfaire.com/global/school.

Makerspaces.com. 2016. "Makerspace Materials." https://www.makerspaces.com/wp-content/uploads/2016/11/Makerspace-Materials-Supply-List.pdf.

Martin, Kim, Mary Compton, and Ryan Hunt. 2017. "Mobile Makerspaces." In *The Makerspace Librarian's Sourcebook*, edited by Ellyssa Kroski, 307–323. Chicago: American Library Association.

Milwaukee Makerspace Wiki. 2017a. "Equipment List." http://wiki.milwaukeemakerspace.org/equipment.

———. 2017b. "Training Checklists." https://wiki.milwaukeemakerspace.org/miscellaneous/training-checklists.

Old Bridge Public Library. 2017. "Idea Farm." http://www.oldbridgelibrary.org/resources/idea-farm.

Rix, Kate. 2014. "Meet the Makers." *Scholastic Administrator*. http://www.scholastic.com/browse/article.jsp?id=3758299.

Smith, Jonathan M. 2017. "Arduino for Librarians." In *The Makerspace Librarian's Sourcebook*, edited by Ellyssa Kroski, 135–155. Chicago: American Library Association.

Tafoya, Stephen M. 2017. "Raspberry Pi for Librarians." In *The Makerspace Librarian's Sourcebook*, edited by Ellyssa Kroski, 113–133. Chicago: American Library Association.

Urban Librarians Council. 2016a. "Bricks and Beer." http://www.urbanlibraries.org/bricks——beer-innovation-1383.php?page_id=530.

———. 2016b. International Seed Library Forum. http://www.urbanlibraries.org/international-al-seed-library-forum-innovation-1348.php?page_id=530.

———. 2016c. "Repair Cafe." http://www.urbanlibraries.org/repair-cafe-innovation-1379.php?page_id=530.

———. 2017. "Makerspaces in Libraries." http://www.urbanlibraries.org/-makerspaces-in-libraries-pages-338.php.

Valenza, Joyce. 2008. "Library as Domestic Metaphor." *Neverending Search* (blog), August 25. http://blogs.slj.com/neverendingsearch/2008/08/25/library-as-domestic-metaphor/.

Wikipedia. 2017a. S.v. "Code.org." https://en.wikipedia.org/wiki/Code.org.

———. 2017b. S.v. "Experiential Learning." https://en.wikipedia.org/wiki/Experiential_learning.

———. 2017c. "LED Art." https://en.wikipedia.org/wiki/LED_art.

———. 2017d. S.v. "Maker Faire." https://en.wikipedia.org/wiki/Maker_Faire.

———. 2017e. S.v. "Open Source Hardware." https://en.wikipedia.org/wiki/Open-source_hardware.

———. 2017f. S.v. "Participatory Culture." https://en.wikipedia.org/wiki/Participatory_culture.

Index

About the Authors

John J. Burke is principal librarian and director of the Gardner-Harvey Library on the Middletown regional campus of Miami University of Ohio. He is former president of the Academic Library Association of Ohio and former chair of the Southwest Ohio Council on Higher Education Library Council.

Ellyssa Kroski is the director of information technology at the New York Law Institute as well as an award-winning editor and author of thirty-six books, including *Law Librarianship in the Digital Age* for which she won the AALL's 2014 Joseph L. Andrews Legal Literature Award. Her ten-book technology series, the Tech Set, won the ALA's Best Book in Library Literature Award in 2011. She is a librarian, an adjunct faculty member at Drexel and San Jose State universities, and an international conference speaker. She was named the winner of the 2017 Library Hi Tech Award from the ALA/LITA for her long-term contributions in the area of library and information science technology and its application.

She can be found at

http://www.amazon.com/author/ellyssa

https://twitter.com/ellyssa

http://www.ellyssakroski.com